THE NEW BIRTH

THE NEW BIRTH
The Nature of Conversion

Austin Phelps
Edited by Paul Dennis Sporer

TARXIEN PRESS

Anza Publishing, Chester, NY 10918
Tarxien Press is an imprint of Anza Publishing
Copyright © 2005 by Anza Publishing

This work is a new, unabridged edition of *The New Birth*, by Austin
Phelps, originally published in 1867.

Library of Congress Cataloging-in-Publication Data
Phelps, Austin, 1820–1890.
   The new birth / Austin Phelps ; editor, Paul D. Sporer.
      p.   cm.
   Includes index.
   ISBN: 1–932490–08–6 (hardcover : alk. paper)
   1. Regeneration (Theology)
   2. Conversion.
   3. Holy Spirit.
I. Sporer, Paul D. II. Title.
BT790.P515 2004
234'.4--dc22   2004015366

Visit AnzaPublishing.com for more information on outstanding
authors and titles. Please support our efforts to restore great literature
to a place of prominence in our culture.

⊚ This book is printed on acid-free paper.

ISBN: 1–932490–08–6 (hardcover)
ISBN: 1–932490–58–2 (softcover)

Contents

Chapter 3
Truth: The Instrument of Regeneration

Chapter 4
Responsibility As Related to Sovereignty

Chapter 5
The Indwelling of the Holy Spirit

Editor's Preface

This work by Austin Phelps goes back to a time when theology was not considered "heavy". It contains an inspirational discussion about conversion, and sees faith as creating new possibilities and accomplishments. In modest, inspiring, but still powerful language, it puts forward many important ideas using a sensible, logical plan that helps the individual interact with God in his new spiritual life. As the title suggests, *The New Birth* views the concept of conversion as a momentous, singular event. Phelps discusses this concept in relation to the subjects of guilt, self-respect, ritual, laws, mysticism, regeneration, the power of truth, the role of the preacher, and responsibility. Phelps strikes just the right balance of advice, admonition, dogma and social commentary. His writing is almost poetic, yet also steady, careful, straightforward and compelling. One reviewer of the original edition had this to say about the book: "It is thoroughly practical, appealing continuously to the religious sensibilities of every reader."

Austin Phelps (1820-1890) was a Congregational clergyman who was also a famous author. Phelps' books are generally speaking devotional, homiletical, and theological in character. *The Still Hour* was published in 1860 in both America and Britain, and became extremely popular, selling some 200,000 copies. He then published a number of works about the complex and varied tasks of a minister: *The Theory of Preaching; Lectures on Homiletics* (1881); *Men and Books; or Studies in Homiletics* (1882); *My Study and Other Essays* (1886) *Rhetoric; Its Theory and Practice* (1895). He also wrote articles for the *Congregationalist*.

We have kept the entire original text, and added an index. This book, originally published in 1866, was directed towards members of the ministry, Sabbath-school teachers, and his fellow Christians, whom he hoped would find useful information which would help them, either "in their own Christian culture or in their efforts to win souls to Christ". He also sincerely desired that the book would assist in the individual's conversion using the "calm reasonings by which they are accustomed to judge of truth in other things."

PAUL DENNIS SPORER

Chapter 1

Conversion: Its Nature

I. THE NECESSITY OF CONVERSION

It was an exaggeration, yet one which contained more of truth than of hyperbole, in which a late writer affirmed that the most characteristic thing this world has to show to other worlds is a scaffold on the morning of an execution. It is true that to a holy mind the distinctive idea in the condition of this world is that of *guilt*. It is not dignity; it is not beauty; it is not wisdom; it is not power; it is *guilt*. It is not weakness; it is not misfortune; it is not suffering; it is not death; it is *guilt*.

·Any thoughtful observer, therefore, must believe that this world needs to be changed, in order to become the dwelling-place of God. No historian, with any just conception of man as he has been and is on the theatre of nations, doubts this. No philosopher with any knowledge of God as he is, doubts this. No man, with any honest insight into his own heart, doubts this necessity of change, to fit man for the presence of God. A seraph hovering over the field of Solferino could scarcely feel a more appalling conviction of this necessity than any individual sinner feels, when his own heart and the idea of God are revealed to his conscience side by side.

Such has been the general belief of the race. They are the few maniacs who have denied it. The great religious systems of the world have been founded upon the conviction that man must be changed. Be the gods what they may, man must be changed, to be at peace with any deity. Our blinded and sickened race has sought to change itself by most laborious and cunning devices. Remorse has been the equivalent of genius in its inventions. By baptismal rites, by anointings, by branding with mysterious symbols, by incantations of magic, by sacred amulets, by ablutions in consecrated rivers; by vigils and abstinences and flagellations, and the purgative of fire; by distortions of conscience in rites of which it is a shame to speak; and by that saddest of all human beliefs, which would doom a human spirit to migrate for millions of years through metamorphoses of bestial and reptile existence,— man has struggled to change himself, that he might be prepared to dwell at last under the pure eye of God. Even those fools who have said in their heart, there is no personal God, have drifted unconsciously in their speculations upon a caricature indeed, and yet a resemblance of this very faith in man's need of a change to make him worthy of the divinity which is within him.

It is impressive to observe how Pantheism, in its wildest freaks, is dragged towards a doctrine of regeneration. The idea haunts it. It speaks in language which a Christian preacher need not refuse in describing the phenomenon of conversion. Its apostles tell us of a certain stage in individual history at which the soul must awake and "bestir itself, and struggle as if in the throes of birth"; that it must "wrestle with doubt, or cower trembling under the wings of mystery"; that it must "search heaven and earth for answers to its questions"; that it must "turn in loathing from the pleasures of sense," under its "irrepressible longings after the good, the true, the beautiful; after freedom, immortality." They tell us of the tumult and torment of this "crisis of internal life." They profess to inform us how the soul may make its way out of this chaos of distress into a "noble, perfect manhood"; how, as one has expressed it, the soul may "once more feel around it the fresh breath of the open sky, and over it the clear smile of heaven; how the streams of thought may again flow on in harmony; how content is to be regained with one's position in the system of things; how all fear and torment are to give place to blessedness; how love is again to suffuse the world, and over every cloud of mystery, to be cast a bow of peace."

Thus, I repeat, the idea of regeneration haunts philosophy in its most impious departures from God. With a God, or without a God, philosophy cannot get away from the sense of the necessity of a change in man to fit him for something to which he is predestined. Put into the language of any philosophy on this subject the two ideas of the Holy Spirit and of sin, and a Christian preacher may adopt the whole of it in his delineation of conversion.

This necessity, therefore, of some great, critical, formative change in man, may be assumed as a truth on which the mind of the race is substantially a unit. On this theme, as on many of the first principles of religion, the wanderings of the human mind from God are forever checked by oceanic currents which draw it inward, and compel it to sail along the coast of truth, never far or long out of sight of the mainland.

What, then, is the nature of that change which man needs to render him an object of divine complacency? Our dependence upon the word of God for the answer is immediate and absolute. Philosophy, independently of the scriptures, has taught the world almost nothing with regard to it. Even theological standards, uninspired, have added nothing to the wisdom of an awakened conscience in a child, except as they have translated the declarations of the word of God. We all wish to know, on a subject like this, not so much what philosophers or theologians have believed as what God has said.

II. Biblical Emblems of Conversion

It will be instructive, then, to recall briefly certain of the representative passages of the Bible which set forth the nature of conversion.

The most familiar of these represent religious conversion by the change which occurs in natural birth. One can almost feel the fascination of the calm, subdued authority with which our Lord taught to his timid pupil the paradox of regeneration: "Except a man be born of water and of the Spirit, he cannot enter into the kingdom of God." "Except a man be born again he cannot see the kingdom of God." "That which is born of the flesh is flesh, and that which is born of the Spirit is spirit." Birth of body—birth of soul! The one stands over against the other, as if for the sake of reflecting each by its resemblance to the other. Then, to check the astonishment excited by the seeming extravagance of his speech, he adds: "Marvel not that I said, Ye must be *born* again." "Marvel not"—this is no cause for dumb amazement; it is but one of the rudiments of truth. Art thou a master in Israel, and knowest not this thing?

A similar boldness of imagery is manifest in that class of passages which represent religious conversion under the figure of a change from death to life. As if birth from non-existence were too natural an emblem to express the whole truth of the anomalous change effected by regeneration, we hear an apostle exclaiming "Awake thou that sleepest, and arise from the dead." "You hath he quickened, who were dead in trespasses and sins." Another, in the assurance of a regenerate experience, declares "We know that we have passed from *death* unto *life.*" Conceive what intensity of significance this metaphor must have had to those of the apostolic age, in which the miracle of resurrection from the tomb was a reality in current history, a fact of common fame!

A similar vividness of contrast is preserved by a third class of passages, which express conversion by the figure of passing from *darkness* to *light*. What is the force of such language as this? "Ye are a chosen generation;" he "hath called you out of darkness into his marvellous light." "Ye were sometimes darkness." Not in darkness only, but darkness itself. Night was the symbol of your very souls. "But now are ye light in the Lord." Not in light, merely, but light itself

"Holy Light—offspring of heaven, first-born."

The noonday is the emblem of your being. Among the most beautiful of the scriptural titles of the regenerate, are these: "children of the light," "children of the day," "saints in light." Some of the most stirring exhortations to renewed men are founded upon this contrast in nature. "Cast off the works of darkness, put on light"—"we are not of the night"—"have no fellowship with the works of darkness"—"what communion hath light with darkness?"

The force of such language is not diminished by a fourth class of passages, which speak of conversion under the figure of a change in the most central organ of physical vitality. "A new heart also will I give you, and a new spirit will I put within you." "I will take away the stony heart." "I will give you a heart of flesh." "Make to you a new heart." A new heart! To this day, what words of wisdom have we learned by which to express a regenerate state more intelligibly or more vividly than by these, which we breathe into the prayers of our children?

But perhaps the climax of the daring imagery of the scriptures on this subject is exceeded in a fifth class of passages, of a literal force, which represent God and Satan as the sovereigns of hostile empires; and the change which man undergoes in conversion is a transfer from the one dominion to the other. Paul did not scruple to affirm his commission to preach a gospel which should "turn men from the power of Satan unto God." "The power of Satan!" This was no fiction of a distempered brain, in an age when demoniacal possession was a common and an acknowledged form of bodily affliction. "The Father hath delivered us from the power of darkness, and hath translated us into the kingdom of his dear Son." "The power of darkness!" This was no feeble image to the thought of an Oriental people, whose faith had filled the night air with demoniac spirits. "In time past ye walked according to the prince of the power of the air. But God, rich in mercy, hath quickened us, hath raised us up, hath made us sit in heavenly places, in Christ Jesus." "Walking according to the prince of the power of the air!" This was no mysticism and no hyperbole to the ancient faith, whose angelology peopled the elements with spiritual intelligences, some of whom swayed the atmosphere malignantly. "The kingdom of Christ" — "the kingdom of the dear Son" — "heavenly places in Christ Jesus"! These were conceptions of unutterable meaning to minds whose only ideal of government was that of absolute empire, and whose thought of obedience was wrapped up in that eternal idea of *loyalty,* in which self is forgotten, and the sovereign of the realm is all in all.

These passages may suffice as a specimen of the methods by which religious conversion is described in the style of inspiration. Yet no possible selection of proof-texts could be the strongest evidence of the scriptural doctrine of regeneration. The climax of proof of such a doctrine is that it pervades the system of biblical teaching. It is one of the constructive ideas of inspiration which are not so much here or there, as everywhere. It is pervasive, like the life-blood in the body. It is like caloric in the globe. If a tortuous exegesis evades it in one passage, it is inevitable in the next. Expel it from a thousand texts, and it remains in secret implications all along the interval pages between them. Wrench it away from every text in which theologians have found it, and its echo still reverberates from one end of the Bible to the other. We can get rid of it, only by flinging away the system of revelation in which it breathes — everywhere present, everywhere needed to complete the symmetry of truth, and, everywhere imperative as an oracle of God.

Our chief inquiry, therefore, should be: What does this language mean in which we are taught man's need of a change to render him a friend of God?

III. Conversion Not a Ritual Change

The scriptural emblems of conversion represent a change of *character*, as distinct from any variety of change by ritual observances. No single conception of religious conversion is more forcibly suggested by the Bible than this — that it is a reality and not a form. If the sole object of the scriptures in their teaching of this doctrine had been to prevent mistake on this point, and to reprove the proneness of the human mind to degrade religious experience to a religious form, their language could scarcely have been more happily adjusted to its object. With this volume in our hands, we do not know how to reason with men who exalt ceremonial ordinances or formulae as substitutes for a change of heart. We must rank among the tokens of intellectual disease, we must regard as a degradation in a civilized mind, that taste which leads one to protrude a Christian baptism, or the imposition of consecrated hands, or the profession of a Christian creed, or communion with a Christian church, or the reception of the Lord's supper, in advance of that work of God's Spirit by which a sinner is born again. It seems like solemn trifling to debate on such a faith. "How readest thou?" is the only query by which we can suggest the remedy for the sickliness of such a mind. To the law and to the testimony! If the scriptural idea of regeneration be definable in any particular of its versatile exhibition here, it surely is so in this, that the change it portrays is independent of external form or symbol. It is an event in spiritual experience. It is a change in the man. The man — the vital, the immortal part of him — feels the change. He lives it. When we pass from this substance of the thing, to consider forms, ordinances, creeds, professions, as distinct from the thing, as its substitutes or its superiors or its constituents, we descend from realities to mimic play-things. These incidents to a religious life indeed lose their significance as symbols even. *They are symbols of nothing.* They are a forgery and a mummery.

In the nature of conversion there is nothing that we know of which should forbid its occurrence in a disembodied state. If we could know that probation encloses the intermediate state of the departed, we might conceive of regeneration in all its majesty as experienced in that land of pure spirits. Without a form to signalize it, without a whisper to proclaim it, there would be joy in heaven. When, therefore, men degrade the dignity of this change to that of an appendage to a ritual; when they overlay its simplicity by imposing upon it burdensome and intricate ordinances; when they overshadow its delicate spirituality by building around and above it even the scriptural symbols which express it, we only speak the uniform language of the scriptures and of common sense, when we catch the tone of an apostle and say — "we do not know whether we have baptized — Christ sent us not for this — lest the cross of Christ should be of no effect."

John Randolph, in a letter to a friend, written at a time when his mind was agitated by religious inquiry, speaks of a volume which he had then before him, and in which it was armed, he says, that "no man is converted without the experience of a miracle." "Such," he continues, "is the substance" of the author's faith: A man "must be sensible of the working of a miracle in his own person. Now, my good friend, I have never experienced anything like this. I have been sensible, and am always, of the proneness to sin in my nature. I have grieved unfeignedly for my manifold transgressions. I have thrown myself upon the mercy of my Redeemer. But I have felt nothing like what this writer requires." "It appears incredible that one so contrite as I sometimes know myself to be should be rejected entirely by infinite mercy." Yet "I fear that I presume upon God's mercy. I sometimes dread that I am in a far worse condition than if I had never heard God's word."

This extract illustrates the method in which minds not accustomed to the technicalities of a theological dialect will often interpret and misinterpret unguarded or confused speech respecting the doctrine of regeneration. It is the legitimate interpretation of any language which degrades conversion from the level of a moral change to that of a change in the constitution of a soul. I say "degrades conversion"; for, what do we mean by a constitutional change? As applied to a spiritual intelligence, a constitutional change is a change either in its essence, or in its susceptibilities, or in its executive powers. But a change in either or all of these is, in respect of the ends of moral government, of less profound significance than a change of character.

The world has been very slow in learning that *miracles are not the grandest disclosure of Omnipotence.*

The material world contains more sublime displays of power than those of miraculous dignity. The sidereal universe, swayed by the forces of law, is a nobler work of God than that in which he said: "Sun stand thou still upon Gibeon; and thou moon, in the valley of Ajalon." In the animal creation there is a grandeur of divine working which no miracle has stamped upon it. The government of animal nature by laws which make it as true to God's will as the line of a bee in its flight, or the swoop of an eagle from its nest, is a more illustrious expression of the divine mind than the piling up of the quails in the wilderness two cubits deep.

So, in the world of mind, law is itself a more majestic thought than that of the suspension of law. The government of an intelligent universe under the law of moral freedom, exhibits a more imperial reach of God's power than the government of such a universe outside of that law. The government of finite mind, speaking anthropologically, is a more august achievement than the creation of that mind. The idea of *character* is an advance upon the idea of *nature*. Character in a soul, conceived of as an effect of God's working, is a more sublime product than the make of that soul. Do you conceive of moral character as something in the constitution of a soul, like the grain of a piece of wood? By such a conception you abase the soul itself, for the purpose of moral government, to a level with a piece of wood. Do you define to yourself depravity as a viciousness ingrained in the very build of a spirit, like the knarl of an oak? By such a definition you precipitate the spirit itself, for the ends of moral government, to a level with the knarl of an oak. Do you imagine gracious affections as inserted into the very nature of a man, as one would infuse a new gas into the atmosphere? By such a fancy you degrade the man himself, for the intents of moral government, to a level with a gas in the atmosphere. Do you describe regeneration as an act which impregnates a sinner's being with a new power, as you would magnetize a piece of steel? By such a description you drag down a sinner's being, for the objects of moral government, to a level with a piece of steel. Omnipotence can no more rule the one than the other by a moral system.

Conversion More than Miracles
Is it, then, to be supposed that such conceptions as these underlie the scriptural emblems of that change which a sinner needs to render him an object of God's complacency? There is in these emblems a height and a depth, a length and a breadth, of significance, which such thoughts of

regeneration and its surroundings in the system of truth do not fill up, and fill out, and fathom to the bottom. By the side of such emblems these thoughts appear sensuous and materialistic. Nothing but a literal interpretation of the language of these emblems can bind them to the sphere of constitutional phenomena. The instant we leave their literal force, — that is, the moment we conceive of them *as emblems* of truth, — truth is buoyant within them. It springs up above the sphere of merely creative power, into that of moral empire, where God makes flexible to his will the immense populations of intelligence and of liberty which fill the universe with his own image. There, man is a man, and not a manikin. A sinner is a sinner, and not a wretch only. He is responsible, self-acting, free; responsible because self-acting; self-acting because free, and free because otherwise moral government over him is a fiction. Conversion being a change in the character of a free sinner, *regeneration,* in respect of its moral solemnity, is something other and more than re-creation. It belongs to another and a loftier plane of Omnipotence.

If anything, more than the natural interpretation of the Scriptures were needed to establish this view — that conversion is a change of character, as distinct from constitutional changes — two simple facts would corroborate this as the necessary interpretation.

Conversion a Fact in Experience

One is, that Christian experience proves no other than a change of character in conversion. Conversion is an experience. It is one of the most ancient and one of the most modern facts in the mental history of this world. Consciousness has taken cognizance of it in unnumbered hearts. Real life has proved it by innumerable tests. Yet no regenerate man knows anything of a re-creation of his nature, or a multiplication of his powers. No Christian is conscious of new faculties. None exhibits such in common life. A converted man thinks, reasons, remembers, imagines now; and he did all these before conversion. A regenerate heart feels, desires, loves, hates, now; and it did all these before. A new-born soul chooses, resolves, plans, executes; and it did all these before. The *chief subjects of thought are changed*—they are revolutionized. The prime objects of love and hatred are changed — they are *transposed.* The supreme inclination of the affections is changed—it is *reversed.* The *character* of the purposes is changed — it is transformed. In these respects, indeed, old things are passed away, and all things are new. But beyond this, neither consciousness nor observation testifies to any other change. No other could add to this any weight of moral significance. The man could have been, so far as we know, no more a Christian, no more an object of complacency to God, no more at peace with his own conscience, if regenerating grace had been a solvent of his nature, and had reduced it to its elements, and reconstructed the man by an improved process of creation.

Conversion a Reasonable Change

The other fact is, that the unregenerate man cannot be made intelligently to feel the reasonableness of God in making salvation dependent on any other change in a sinner than a change of character. The way of salvation is urged upon the acceptance of men, in the Bible, as a reasonable way. God lays open the whole subject, as our Lord did to Nicodemus, as one which is susceptible of reasonable defence. It is to be presumed to be capable of seeming reasonable to an unregenerate mind. The revelation of the mind of God on the subject is addressed to an unregenerate world. Its appeal is to the good sense of men—that sum total of the intellectual virtues equipoised and symmetrical. "Marvel not" —"Come, let us reason together"—"Are not my ways equal? saith the Lord"—"What more could I do to my vineyard that I have not done in it?"—"O fools, and slow of heart to believe." Such is the tone of inspiration in exposing its great organic truths to the test of reason.

But the theory of the necessity of any other change in a sinner than a change of character, as the condition of salvation, does not bear this scrutiny of the good sense of men. A sinner's conscience does not respond to it reasonably; his reason does not respond to it conscientiously. Therefore, it does not deepen his conviction of guilt intelligently. If he reasons consistently upon it,—and some minds will reason consistently here, to their own hurt,—if he reasons consistently upon it, the inevitable inference from it seems to be that he has no responsibility respecting his soul's salvation until regeneration has been performed upon him. I cannot rid myself of a sense of sin; guilt seems to burn within me, like an unearthly fire; yet in reason, with this view of conversion, I cannot see myself to be any more responsible for sin than for my shadow. I feel guilt to be my character, and the whole of it; but in reason, upon this theory, it seems to be my organism only. I feel the burden of sin as if I were its creator, and yet in reason, with this conception of it, it seems to have been born with me by no act of mine. Then by whose act? I feel the unworthiness of my depravity; I am speechless as if I deserved to be damned for it, and yet in reason, with this view of it, the very marrow of my bones seems to be as much responsible for it as the immortal part of me. Then, when by reason I pursue the phantom which yet I feel to be no phantom, where do I find its last refuge? Where is the crime lodged of originating the thing for which I am damned? Yet shall not the Judge of all the earth do right?

That is an awful antagonism—it seems irreverent to conceive of it—in which a sinner's conscience and reason are thus arrayed in conflict, the one condemning him, the other accusing God. It is more than a "conflict of ages." Under the theory before us, it would be the conflict of eternity. Unregenerate mind in the agitations of such unnatural warfare, with unregenerate passions boiling over under the inevitable sense of injustice, cannot be reasoned with. You might as well reason with Vesuvius. That soul can be made to feel helpless, hopeless, reckless; but in reason, that will be the helplessness, the hopelessness, the recklessness of a victim, not a sinner. We may silence the victim. We may overwhelm him with arguments which he cannot answer. We may overawe him with learned and abstruse conjectures. We may teach him what the wise men have recorded of the pre-existence of souls; and his soul may be troubled because he cannot disprove it. We may discourse to him of his personality in Adam, his participation in the Fall, his taste of the forbidden tree; and he may be speechless because he cannot conceive of it, and because, if he should speak, he could only say; "This is my infirmity, that I cannot remember Eden; it is not so much to me, even, as a dream when one awaketh." We may expound to him the "federal representation," and the "imputation of sin"; and, for a moment, he may impute it as a sin to his soul that he cannot help shuddering at the shock which that conception gives to the conscience with which Adam has endued him! We may weigh him down with theologic definitions and qualifications and distinctions, and may back these up with authorities and catechisms, till, through his sheer bewilderment at our prodigious learning, his faith may be held bound by our dogma, like mercury compressed in a globe. But the instant the theologic weights are taken off, the globe flies open, and the prisoner springs out into the free air. Once more in his right mind, his faith falls back to the logic of common sense, and he feels as John

Randolph did, that, on such a theory of depravity, if regeneration means anything, it means that conversion is a miracle. He has no more to do with it than he had with his birth. Then the eternal conflict in his nature — conscience on this side, and reason on that side — breaks out with redoubled rage. Conscience thunders, "There is no peace saith my God to the wicked." Reason flings back in defiant answer, "There is no peace saith my God to the victim."

Constitutional Conversion Not a Duty

The doctrine of a constitutional change in conversion is seldom, if ever, consistently preached. It cannot be thus preached by a man who is intent on results in real life. I may hold it as a theorem, but I cannot preach it. I may defend it as a thesis among theologians, but I cannot press it home upon men from the pulpit. I cannot preach it to careless sinners. I cannot preach it to awakened inquirers. No man can preach it to an audience of anxious men who are seeking after God. No man can preach it in a revival of religion. There is something which stifles it in the very atmosphere of the place in which earnest men have come together, to ask what they must do to be saved.

One preacher of distinction in our own country, during the early part of the present century, who thought that he held this view of regeneration, very consistently acknowledged that he could not preach to impenitent men in a revival of religion. He could preach, and, as some of his published discourses prove, with great power to professing Christians on themes of Christian experience, but he could not preach to unregenerate hearers at a time when they felt salvation to be a present business, and the business of an emergency. On one occasion, when invited to preach at such a time by Professor Stuart, then a pastor in New Haven, he declined the service, and, with tearful eyes, assigned as his reason that his preaching was not adapted to the demands of such scenes as he had witnessed there. He could not adjust to them his views of the nature of a change of heart. A revival was an emergency for which no provision was found in his theory of the way in which the gospel should be preached to unregenerate men. Was not such a confession the strongest possible corroborative evidence that he had mistaken the doctrine of the scriptures?

We cannot err, then, in adopting as one of the first principles of revelation on the subject of the new birth, that it is a change of character, as distinct from constitutional changes in the soul. It is a change in that, and only that, for which conscience and reason, reason and conscience, hold a man responsible, as for a thing of his own originating and his own nurturing.

V. CONVERSION NOT A MYSTICAL CHANGE

Some doctrines of the Scriptures are so clear that their very perspicuity is their vindication. A statement of them amounts to proof. Other doctrines are so mysterious that statement and testimony are all the evidence we can have of their truthfulness. We can reason upon them no further than to observe that their statement is not internally a contradiction, and that the testimony which supports them is authoritative. But there are other truths in which the mysterious and the intelligible are so interwoven that to an unpractised eye they may seem inseparable. Such a truth is that of regeneration.

On the one hand, what God's working in the change of a sinner's heart is, as distinct from the effect of that working, in other words, what regeneration is, as distinct from conversion, who can tell? We know scarcely more of the interior of the work of God in regenerating a soul than we do of the mechanic power in creating a soul. The dynamics of the phenomenon elude all our philosophy. When Coleridge said, "By what manner of working God changes a soul from evil to good, how he impregnates the barren rock with gems and gold, is to the human mind an impenetrable mystery in all cases alike," he uttered only what every thoughtful mind feels. Thus our Lord taught to Nicodemus: The wind bloweth where it listeth, but the whence and the whither ye cannot tell; so is everyone that is born of the Spirit. But this is very far from affirming that the change itself, the result of God's working, is an enigma. A change of character, in itself considered, is one of the most intelligible of historic facts. It is like a transparency in the sun. It has the *simplicity of contrast*. It is like a change from "yes" to "no," from "no" to "yes."

Yet an inquiring mind sometimes suffers confusion from permitting the mysteriousness of the methods of regeneration to overspread the crystalline character of the fact of conversion. The idea seems often to be entertained that this change itself is the great secret of Christian experience. An unregenerate mind cannot know what it is, any more than how it is. It appears, in the view of some minds, to bar the entrance to the church, like the watchword of a brotherhood, to which, from the outside, none can be initiated. Said one, in deep anguish, to a pastor, "I do not understand it. I do not comprehend what I must do, or what I must be. I seem to myself to be doing all I can do. I am not conscious of hostility to God. I long to accept Christ and him only as my Saviour. What more is requisite to give me the peace which others feel, I do not know. The mystery of the thing shuts me in. Yet guilt weighs upon me like the hills. I feel as if I were buried alive."

The state of mind expressed in this language is, in more respects than one, unnatural and unscriptural. It is not an experience to which men are ever exhorted, or invited, or intimidated, in the Bible. But the point of its erroneousness which demands notice here is that of its confounding a change of heart with the divine methods which induce the change, and conceiving the one to be as enigmatical as the other. This is like confounding light with the voice which said: "Let there be light." An inquiring sinner wrongs his own soul, and distrusts the Saviour's heart towards him, when he lingers in dumb anguish before the cross, hoping that he shall eventually understand the subject of conversion, and thus be enabled to become a Christian. To a sinner in the condition which I here imagine, there is nothing further to be understood in order to his salvation. There is no abyss of mystery to be fathomed. He has the truth, and the whole of it. How does our Lord address Nicodemus in this condition of purblind anxiety? He chides him, as one would a child whose knowledge was needlessly beneath his years. Art thou a master in Israel, and knowest not these things?

These emblems of conversion, too — what boldness of contrast pervades them all! When we mean to express an idea with indubitable clearness, we seek the aid of contrasted images. We have no difficulty in distinguishing ice and fire. We never mistake the fall of thistle-down for the tread of an elephant. Nothing else reveals midnight like a flash of lightning. So the inspired mind paints the reality of a change of heart by depicting the two states of character between which the change occurs. It is from non-existence to being; from a heart of stone to a heart of flesh; from darkness to light; from death to life; from the empire of fiends to the kingdom of Christ. There is a meaning in such intense symbols of the truth which is meant to be as intensely understood. An

unregenerate mind can understand them. No other difference exists between regenerate and unregenerate perception of the truth in them than
that which divides the knowledge of experience and the knowledge of
theory on all other subjects. A sinner—an unregenerate sinner—a sinner
who feels his own desert of hell — the chief of sinners — may come
before God with none but reasonable fears, none but intelligent convictions, none but manly yearnings after peace, and in conscious helplessness may ask of God, "What shall I do to be saved?" It is a reasonable
inquiry. God will not mock him in the answer. God will not say to him,
"It is a mystery: it is the great secret of the universe. Thy destiny is
unsearchable by thy dim eye. Be still, and know that I am God. Go thy
way for this time; when I have a convenient season I will call thee with
an effectual calling. Go — go thy way." Sinners often treat the Saviour
thus; he is never so merciless to them.

Certain couplets in a very precious hymn, expressive of the sinner's
last resolve, though they are true to a sinner's desponding experience,
still are not worthy, because that experience is not worthy, of the riches
and the freedom of God's grace.

"I'll go to Jesus"

I'll to the gracious King approach
　Whose sceptre pardon gives;
Perhaps he will command my touch,
　And then the suppliant lives.
Perhaps he will admit my plea,
　Perhaps he will hear my prayer!

There is no "perhaps" in God's promises. There is no stammering
speech in God's invitations to an inquiring sinner. There is no hesitancy
of love in God's offers of regenerating grace. More honorable to the truth
as it is in Jesus is the language of adoring trust:

Just as I am — without one plea,
But that thy blood was shed for me.
Just as I am — and waiting not.
Just as I am — though tossed about
With many a conflict.
Just as I am — poor, wretched, blind.
Just as I am — thou *wilt* receive,

Wilt welcome, pardon, cleanse, relieve.
Because thy promise I believe;
   O Lamb of God, I come.

VI. CONVERSION A RADICAL CHANGE

The most characteristic feature in the scriptural view of the nature of
conversion is, that, in distinction from every variety of secondary change,
it is the most radical change of which human character is susceptible.
This conception of the radical nature of conversion is involved in all the
scriptural statements of its necessity, and specially, in the scriptural
metaphors by which it is symbolized. Indeed, the conception with which
the inspired mind appears to have struggled most sturdily under the
poverty of language, was this of the greatness of the change. What else
is signified by the frequency with which the inspired thought forsakes
literal speech, and falls back upon such startling and unqualified metaphors as the creation of light; the resurrection from the dead; the mysterious and unknown change of birth; and translation from the realms of
the prince of the power of the air? Sane minds do not employ such emblems of thought recklessly. We cannot suppose inspiration to prompt
extravagant speech. This is but the sobriety of human dialect, crowded
with and struggling to encompass the magnitude of divine thought.
Scriptural utterances on this subject exhibit the same evidence of the
conflict of truth with the feebleness of language—I had almost said the
impatience of truth at the imbecility of language—which we find in the
scriptural modes of representing the being and majesty of God. Truth,
in the one case as in the other, seems to weigh down the most elastic
tongue, and to exhaust the most voluminous vocabulary, and to search
through the inventions of the most creative imagination, and to pass
from one emblem to another, from one kingdom of resemblances to a
second, till, by the mysteriousness of its drapery, we are compelled to
feel that the naked truth, as appreciated by the mind of God, surpasses
our reach of expression. We can only exclaim, "Eye hath not seer, nor
ear heard it." We cannot define the greatness of the change in literal
speech, otherwise than by pronouncing it the most profound, so far as
we can know, that human nature can experience.

What the birth of the body is to the consciousness of the mind that
inhabits it we do not know; but, for its significance to the moral govern-

ment of God over the mind, it cannot be so momentous a change as that mind's conversion. What disembodiment at death is to the experience of the spirit which thus goes out into an unexplored eternity we cannot conceive; but, in respect of the solemnity of moral government, it cannot be of such magnitude as the regeneration of that spirit. What the resurrection of the body is to the history of the soul which has been again enrobed in it we cannot conjecture; but, in its relation to the moral government of that soul, it cannot be so elemental a change as that soul's conversion. Such physical transformations and transitions can be hints only, and feeble hints, of the spiritual phenomenon which transcends them.

Counterfeits of Conversion

Let us then, for our practical instruction, observe several mental and moral changes with which conversion is often confounded. Observe, briefly, that a change of external deportment is not the chief result of regeneration. No matter how pervasive that change may be, it can bear no comparison with religious conversion. When a man who has been addicted to sensual vice becomes a sober man, a chaste man, an industrious man, a good citizen, a kind father, brother, son, there is a notable change. It is a real change in character. It is a change for which a man deserves to be respected. But that is not a change which fills up the language of the Scriptures in designating the translation of a man into the kingdom of God. In other words, conversion and reformation are not synonymous.

Again, no increase of seriousness of mental habit is synonymous with religious conversion. A young man often experiences, as the natural result of expanding intellect, an increase of thoughtfulness. When he was a child he thought as a child; now he has put away childish things. Manly thought awakens manly sensibility. He acquires some sense of the reality of life as a conflict. A certain dignity of character is formed, which is as natural a growth of manhood upon the stock of youth as the addition of a cubit to the stature of an infant. It is indeed a valuable change, a change necessary to success in life, a change which will command respect, as it deserves respect; but it is not conversion. No growth of earnestness is synonymous with that new birth which a soul experiences under the regenerating act of God.

Further, the abandonment of any single passion does not constitute conversion. Such a change as this often occurs as the fruit of increasing years. Often the effect is to mellow a man's character, by substituting for a turbulent vice one more mild and comely, and yet a vice as deeply seated, as odious to God. Warren Hastings, after his ambition had burnt itself out in India, realized the favorite dream of his youth, by returning to spend his old age in the homestead where his ancestors had lived in luxury. Here was a change, indeed. It must have involved in some sort a change in character. It was an abandonment of a fiery passion for a harmless indulgence of an aged man's love of repose. But this obviously is no such change as the word of God portrays by the emblem of the dawn of light on a benighted wanderer.

Once more, conversion is not the development of character by natural germination in the heart. Character often undergoes a change by which qualities long concealed spring to light under a change of circumstance. Traits of generous manhood, the germs of which have been repressed, shoot up thriftily under improved discipline. Energies which have slumbered are roused by emergencies. No man knows the compass of his own nature till it has been distended by some great sorrow or great opportunity for achievement. Such facts in life tempt us to self-conceit respecting the hidden nobleness of man. Much of the religion of literature is founded upon the idea of concealed virtue. A divinity is imagined to dwell within us, and to be awaiting only the incitement of occasion or the felicity of circumstance to develop itself in all that man should desire or respect in character. Yet no such change as this can be the complement of the scriptural conception of that revulsion of character which is no less than resurrection from the dead.

What a satire on developed goodness in man is expressed in the tone of the Scriptures towards the best embodiment of the natural virtues! Breathe into Nature's good man the most comely of her graces; educate in him the most refined of her sensibilities; develop in him the most magnanimous of her impulses; fashion in him the most docile obedience to her teachings; nurture in him the most elegant and placid of her tastes so that to the silken judgment of the world his character shall seem to be a paragon of beauty, — "fair as a star when only one is shining in the sky"; yet if that fascinating being—that young man of whom it shall be said that Jesus, beholding him, loved him—has not been changed by the washing of regeneration and the renewing of the Holy Ghost, the honest eye of God sees him as a naked soul in bondage to the prince of the power of the air.

A Converted Man—A New Man

If the scriptural dialect on this subject means anything, it must indicate that conversion is a change which brings into existence a character which had no being before. Does not birth introduce to a new existence? Is life only a development of nonentity? Is vitality a germination of the life of a corpse? Is light a growth of the midnight? Is the kingdom of God a superstructure upon the kingdom of Satan? If development, growth, germination, are the things in which regeneration exhibits itself, we need no such emblems as these to express it. They are out of character and out of place. They are untruthful. The Scriptures are full of puerile extravagances and grimaces of diction. There is no propriety in recognizing two classes of mankind, such as the Scriptures separate by a gulf of fire. There are no such beings as sinners and saints, — enemies of God and friends of God,—natural men and spiritual men,—men who are in darkness and men who are in light, — men who are dead and men who are alive,—men who are in God's kingdom and men who are in Satan's kingdom. These are unreal and unjust distinctions. Men are all of one class. They differ not in kind, but in degree of character. Here, then, we have a large and varied class of descriptions, uttered by the Spirit of God of men and to men, to which among men we find no counterpart in reality. But one half of the Bible is apposite to this world. Is this credible? The development, then, of an existing germ of holiness is not the scriptural idea of a change of heart. In other words, no process of self-culture can be equivalent in its fruits to the divine act of regeneration.

Character under a Law of Perpetuity

The radical nature of conversion may be still further illustrated, by observing for a moment a principle which we often lose sight of in meditation upon this theme, but which lies at the bottom of all genuine notions of man as a subject of government. It is that character itself has *fixedness*. In the profound and ultimate sense in which we employ the term to indicate what a soul is as a subject of moral government, character has an element which approaches immutability. Character, good or bad, once formed, tends to perpetuate itself. Once in it, a soul grows to it, and rises or sinks with it. The necessity of creating a character is the most transcendent privilege, and at the same time the most appalling peril, of a moral being. The law of perpetuity is deep-laid in its very nature. By this law a moral being tends to be always what it has been and is. It is this which renders guilt so fearful. The law of guilt is to perpetuate guilt. "Once a sinner, always a sinner," expresses the tendency of fallen mind.

A truth is enveloped in those forms of expression which eminent and holy men have often used to express depravity, when they have spoken of "a sinful nature"; of "a depraved constitution"; of a "helpless corruption"; of "inability to repent." Much as these modes of expression are misconstrued, and much as they need qualification, there is still a truth in them. The use of them often indicates the struggle of a pious heart to express that truth. They are not without resemblance to some of the forms of scriptural phraseology. They have their counterpart in the common usage of men in figurative speech. The truth they express is that of the natural fixedness of character in a sinner's heart. On the principle of the tendency of all character to perpetuate itself, a sinner's character is fixed. What he has once made it, its tendency is to be forever. That it will be forever, unless the power of God be interposed to reverse it.

True, we do not conceive of this as an invincible tendency. It exists by no compulsory law. It asserts, therefore, no fatal authority. *It is not a destiny.* We do not reason upon the laws of character as we reason upon the laws of matter, or even as we reason upon laws of intellect, as intellect only. Character, in the ultimate conception of it as a moral phenomenon, is unique. It is not a metal; it is not a mind. It has laws of its own. Its laws are but the expression of the human mind which creates it, as the laws of light are an expression of the divine mind which created that; as the laws of intellect are an expression of the infinite Intelligence in whose image it is made. When, therefore, we apply the term "nature" to character we cannot mean by it the same thing as when we speak of the "nature" of silver or the "nature" of memory. We must not confound the laws of character with the emblems of these laws, which we sometimes seek for in the laws of matter and in the organic laws of mind. Matter and mind are God's creation. Human character is man's creation. The creative power is as absolute in the one case as in the other. God rules finite character not by creation, but by government. He governs it as *character,* not as the wind or as the springs of the sea.

Yet, after all, such is this imperial will of man, by which it is his privilege and his peril to be what he will, that a pressure towards immutability grows out of its nature and accumulates with time. Once bent one way, the spring coils itself that way forever. Once set in the chosen mould, the compound indurates into granite. Such is character in the ultimate notion of it. A creation by man's own act—a free creation—a creation which can be reversed, yet once in being, it tends to deathless being like that of God. It is a start on a journey into eternity, in a direction from which, but by God's interposition, no traveller returns. It is in the light of such a conception of the awful immortality of character that we must judge of the radical nature of its change in conversion.

The Supreme Change

It remains, then, to observe, that there is but one change of character conceivable which shall meet all the peculiarities affirmed of religious conversion. It is the change from sin to holiness. It is a change from absolute sin to the first dawn of holiness in the soul. It is that unique change which has no parallel and no adequate similitude, in which an intelligent mind, a free mind, a self-acting mind, a mind which has intelligently, freely, of its own will, abandoned God, is led for the first time in its moral history by Almighty grace to return, and give itself to God. For the first time, then, a sinner appreciates God. For the first time he loves God. For the first time he chooses God. For the first time he enjoys God. For the first time he is born of God. For the first time his life is hid with Christ in God. God, *God,* GOD, is the one being to whom his soul mounts up, and in whom he enters into rest. He may be flooded with joy unspeakable, because he is engulfed in the blessedness of GOD.

Chapter 2

Regeneration:
The Work of God

An unperverted mind will approach reverently any revelation of God in the destiny of man. The conception of an invisible Power has itself a fascination for a finite mind. It is not strange that the Wind should have been deified in pagan theology. Little as a human mind can know of a power which the eye has never seen, yet when dependence upon such a power reaches out to cover everything in the future which renders immortality attractive, a sense of mingled grandeur and suspense is awakened, which holds the mind fast, in the attitude of a subdued and anxious learner.

Metaphysical relations of truth in such connections are often unwelcome. Sometimes, indeed, they seem unnatural. The instinct of a docile spirit is to approach such truths as objects of faith, rather than as subjects of analysis.

To no theme is such a spirit more becoming than to the revealed fact that *the change of a human heart is the work of God.*

I. DIVINE SOVEREIGNTY IN REGENERATION

We shall reach the most vital aspects of this subject most directly by first defining, to ourselves, briefly, what we mean when we ascribe the change of a man's heart to Divine Power. This doctrine may be considered as affirming several truths.

In the first place, it affirms that a human soul never changes its own character from sin to holiness through the involuntary development of its own sensibilities. Holiness cannot so exist in emotive forms as to spring up impulsively in a heart which is unconscious of will to produce it. Holiness is not an instinct. It does not grow automatically out of the make of the soul, as, with proper incitements, compassion, gratitude, reverence, may do. The heart of man, in relation to the causes of rectitude within it, is not like a harp, which to utter its voices needs only to be hung in the wind.

The doctrine we are to consider further affirms that man never turns from sin to holiness by an effort of his own will, independent of super-natural Power. This is something more than the assertion often made, "that man cannot change his own affections by direct volition." The inability involved in this latter assertion is not the fruit of depravity. The grace of God does not remove it. It lies in the constitution of mind, re-generate or unregenerate. A saint cannot, more than a sinner, love God by resolving "I will love God." Either might as reasonably resolve: "I will see this symphony of Beethoven; I will hear the beauty of Loch Lomond." The blind man had more of reason in his philosophy when he pro-nounced the color of scarlet to be like the sound of a trumpet.

The doctrine of man's dependence upon God for regeneration affirms nothing respecting such psychological possibilities of change. It affirms that man never turns from sin to holiness by any effort, direct or indirect, of his own will, uninfluenced by supernatural power. We do not affirm that he cannot do this, except in the figurative sense in which a mother cannot hate her infant; a compassionate man cannot bear the sight of a victim on the rack; a miser cannot part with his gold; Joseph's brethren could not speak peaceably unto him; God cannot lie. In the literal sense of both scientific and popular speech, a sinner can, but will not, cease to be a sinner without the intervention of Divine Power.

Consistently with this view, the doctrine of Divine agency in regenera-tion also affirms that the unaided force of truth does not suffice to per-suade the human soul from sin to holiness. Here also we affirm only the fact of experience. The doctrine does not degrade the dignity of truth. It does not deny the intrinsic power of truth over mind as mind, regener-ate or unregenerate. It does not refuse to discern in truth a tendency to convert a soul, and in the soul a tendency to yield to truth. It only affirms the fact of real life, that these tendencies are overborne. The suasive working of truth, when not energized by the grace of God, is a failure.

In this view is involved a subsidiary fact,—that all human instrumen-talities and expedients by which truth is intensified, and so made appre-ciable by human sensibilities, are powerless to change the heart. Author-ity, sympathy, reasoning, eloquence, the magnetism of person, and whatever else enters into the mystery of persuasion, in which mind

impels mind by the enginery of speech, may change well-nigh everything
in man except his character. That, these auxiliaries to truth all fall short
of, in their profoundest reach.

Let it be observed, then, once more, that when we ascribe to God the
change which takes place in regeneration, we mean that, over and above
all natural tendencies and finite agencies, God performs an act of sovereign power in every change of character from sin to holiness. What that
act is, what that power is, other than as characterized by their effects,
the Scriptures do not teach, and we need not affirm.

The psychological process of which moral conversion is the consequence is at best a theme of philosophical conjecture. Belief respecting
it is no necessary part of faith in the biblical doctrine of regeneration.
Beyond a declaration of the fact, we are not called upon to affirm or
deny.

II. Regeneration a Solitary Disclosure of God

Our conception of the fact of divine agency in regeneration may be
sharpened, however, and we may be protected against some confusion
of faith, if we observe that, so far as we know, the act of renewing the
human heart is an entirely unique disclosure of God. We know of nothing
else like it in the history of the universe. We call it "creation." We pray
with the Psalmist, "Create in me a clean heart!" Yet it is not an act of
physical omnipotence, like that which creates an oak. We denominate
this mysterious transformation "a new birth." Yet we should deserve the
rebuke which our Lord gave to Nicodemus, if we should discern in the
act such an expression of omnipotence as that which creates a soul. We
picture this divine renewal as a change of heart." We pray that the stony
heart may be taken and the heart of flesh given. But ours would be a
childish dream of heaven, if we should look for such a miracle of power
as God wrought in the creation of the first woman. God cannot create
a human character as he creates the being who sustains that character.
God could not have created Adam's character as he created Adam. We
speak loosely when we say in our creeds "man was created holy." So, infinite sovereignty could not have originated the piety of the beloved
disciple as it summoned into being the fisherman of Galilee. We portray
this unspeakable change as a "resurrection." We cry out in our despair,

"Who shall deliver us from the body of this death?" But our despair must be eternal, if we have no other hope than such an act of Deity as the raising of Lazarus. The dry bones which Ezekiel saw were in vision only. So far as we know the history of God's working, regeneration stands alone. Divine forces in nature — even divine forces above nature, yet acting upon things material — present no parallels to it.

Consequently the emblems which we derive from the material and the sentient world to express the phenomenon of regeneration are only emblems. They are not kindred facts. They do not belong to the same plane of divine efficiency. They are not *definitions,* they are pictorial *descriptions,* of the new birth. The new birth transcends them, as matter sentient transcends matter inert; as intelligence transcends both; and as character transcends all organism of matter or mind. We shall often conceive most truthfully of such a phenomenon by throwing our minds back of the symbols devised for its expression. As a disclosure of God, it is at once original, solitary, and ultimate. Nothing like it, so far as our knowledge extends, has preceded, or will follow, the earthly history of man. Nothing like it in the universe, so far as revealed to us, lies outside of the moral experience of the human soul. Such a phenomenon, and the primary Cause of it, cannot be exhaustively expressed by any similitude. They must be described by results, rather than defined by analysis. To whom will ye liken God?

It may aid us further to conceive of the regenerating act as a unique disclosure of God's power, if we recall the fact that in like manner we conceive of the atonement as a solitary device of his moral government. Thus, also, we look upon the incarnation as an unparalleled expression of the personality of Godhead. It would be as truthful to confound these with the emblems by which we struggle with our poverty of speech to express them, as it is to confound the regenerating power, as is sometimes done, with creative power, or preserving power, or the power of miracle, or any other variety of executive energy emanating from the Will of God.

Yet if we observe faithfully the actual working of God in regeneration, and judge the cause by its effects, we are not left without some practical hints of its nature.

Thus we approximate a radical idea of it when we discover it to be a moral, as distinct from a physical, power. We have a valuable notion of

it, when we term it persuasive, as distinct from compulsory, in its operation. We derive fearful admonition from the fact that it is resistible, not
invincible, by the subjects of it. Yet we rest in hope when we know that
it is certain in its working, and sure of its end; not capricious, not chime-
rical. And do we not revere the supernatural majesty of it when we look
up to the height of the solitude in which it works, without equal and
without adequate symbol among all the revelations made to us of Infinite
Mind?

III. BIBLICAL VIEW OF SUPERNATURAL IN NEW BIRTH

The proof of the fact of Divine Agency in regeneration is derived
chiefly from the Word of God. An analysis of a single text may serve as
a specimen of the declarative passages in which this truth is taught.

"To as many as received him, to them gave he power to become the
sons of God; which were born not of blood, nor of the will of the flesh,
nor of the will of man, but of God." We cannot press to the quick the
significance of the word "power" here. Yet we need not shrink from it
through fear of its implication against human freedom. We must con-
cede, however, to an objector against the whole conception of a new
birth, that there is here an infelicity, though not necessarily an inaccu-
racy, in our English version. "Prerogative" is the idea which the word in
its connection requires, rather than "ability." "Privilege" it is rendered in
the margin of our larger Bibles. "To them he assigned the privilege of
being the sons of God." But this is not the vital part of the passage in
respect to the truth before us. That appears in the sequel "Which were
born not of blood, nor of the will of the flesh, nor of the will of man, but
of God." That is, this new birth, which entitles men the sons of God, is
not the fruit of ancestral dignity. It is not consequent upon the laws of
natural generation. It is not the product of human influence. It is a work
of God. The language could not be more explicit.

A most interesting feature of the scriptural method of teaching this
truth is seen in the fact that no timidity is exhibited by inspired minds
in their guardianship of it. They do not seem to fear that a change of
heart will not be ascribed to God by those who experience that change.
The passages are not numerous in which the central point of significance
is a contrast of Divine with human power. Occasionally, indeed, we read

of such monitory words as these "By grace ye are saved, through faith, and that not of yourselves — it is the gift of God"; and such as these: "I have planted and Apollos watered, but God gave the increase; so then neither is he that planteth anything, nor he that watereth, but God."

Such, however, is not the general mood of inspiration on this subject. More frequently than otherwise, the fact of the divinity of regeneration is inserted, as if incidentally; not as intrinsically inferior, yet as relatively subordinate, in the structure of the inspired thought. Thus, we are told that "God hath quickened us together with Christ"; the dignity of association with Christ being the gleaming point in the language. We are taught that "as many as are led by the Spirit of God, they are the sons of God"; with emphasis not chiefly on the guidance of the Holy Spirit, but upon the dignity of the adoption. We are admonished, "God hath, from the beginning, chosen you to salvation, through the sanctification of the Holy Ghost"; in which not so much the divinity of the power as the eternity of the election is the focal thought. We are reminded, "Ye are washed, ye are sanctified by the Spirit of our God"; and not so much the agency of the change, as the contrast it has created with "thieves and drunkards and extortioners," marks the climax of impression. We hear Paul exclaiming, "What is the exceeding greatness of the power of God to us who believe"; not the bald fact that it is the power of God, but the unutterable magnitude of that power is the point of concentration.

Thus, the inspired mind speaks at its ease of the fact of Divine working in regeneration, as if it were a truth which an experience of the change, or even an admission of the necessity of the change, would draw after it as an inevitable corollary. Inspiration does not pet the doctrine, nor prop the doctrine, nor seem to tremble for the honor of the doctrine. It treats the doctrine more regally. By collateral mention of it, by calm assumption of it, by cool implications of it, by unpremeditated allusions to it, and by delicate hints of it, the inspired mind treats it as if it were a truth of which an intimation is equivalent to a demonstration; a truth which, once insinuated into the mind through crevices of thought, will be like light to the universe. It will assert itself. It will prove itself. It will vindicate its own dignity, and flood all things else with its superabounding radiance. Such is the temper of the faith in this doctrine which the inspired writers would create in a believing soul. Theirs is a placid faith, an intrepid faith, an unsuspicious faith; a faith never wavering in itself, never tremulous over the treasure it guards; a faith which sees God so intensely in the wonders of his grace, that to its clear, calm eye this world seems like a "drop of water resting in the hollow of Jehovah's hand."

IV. Experience Suggests a Supernatural Cause

We see in the material world much which is immediately suggestive to us of the presence of God. We obtain our first vivid conceptions of Divine power from the evidence of that power in natural phenomena, over which we do not consciously pause to elaborate the conviction of God's working. We do not educe it from a nice balancing of probabilities. We see it; it forces itself upon us. We know it; it overpowers our consciousness of all speculative processes. We can only look on in silent awe while the wonderful perfections of God unfold themselves. Do we not thus see God in a cataract, in a tempest, in the lightning, in the ocean? Do we not thus discern his hand in the heavens, which are the work of his fingers? Do we not thus behold the light of his countenance in the dawn of morning? Do we not thus hear the sound of his footfall when night settles on the world? To a believing spirit these phenomena are all immediately suggestive of God.

Our present inquiry, then, is: Do we discover in the developments of the human soul in that process of experience of which conversion is the exponent any similar tokens of God's agency? Do we perceive anything which impels us to feel, as by intuition, that we are witnessing an act of God?

That every instance of conversion is of this electric character, we cannot affirm. Not every work of God in the natural world is such. God acts in the formation of a vein of anthracite as efficiently as in the creation of the Himalayas. Science teaches us that the forces antecedent in the one case were as elemental and convulsive as those in the other. So in the spiritual world, the change of a soul in regeneration may be wrought by processes which conceal themselves from all eyes but that of Him who sees where is the vein for silver and the place for gold. Yet to the wisdom of a later world those processes shall be seen to have been as formative and as revolutionary as any that have racked other natures with tumultuous conversion.

But some phenomena are observable in the experience of some minds which, assuming the scriptural theory of regeneration as a possible fact, are immediate tokens of the presence and the power of God. To some of these let us direct our thoughts.

God Is Sometimes Suggested by the Manner of Conversion

Of this, illustration will be more convincing than abstract proof. Take, for example, the conversion of the Apostle Paul. Look at it as a fact in the history of mind. Set aside, as irrelevant to the object before us, whatever was miraculous in the events of that journey to Damascus. Make no account of the supernatural light, the voice from heaven, the shock of blindness. Consider not the means, but the manner, of that change in the man. Mark its impetuosity. Note the instantaneousness of that arrest of passion. It is like a torrent frozen in mid-air. Observe the revulsion of feeling. Threatening and slaughter give place to convictions of sin. Malignity is supplanted by prayer. Perceive the revolution of character in that instant of trembling and astonishment. Call it regeneration, conversion, new birth, or by titles more comely to philosophic taste; call it what you will, it is a change of character. The Pharisee becomes a penitent. The persecutor becomes a Christian. The murderer becomes a saint. For aught that appears in the narrative, the change is almost like a flash of lightning. How brief the colloquy which proclaims the whole of it! "Who art thou, Lord?" "I am Jesus." "Lord, what wilt thou have me to do?" We do not know that mind can move more rapidly than this in such a juncture of its history, and yet move intelligently. Then put together the two lives of the man—his life before, and his life after, this convulsive crisis. Saul and Paul join hands over this invisible gulf, as over the river of death—the same being, yet two different men. His character has experienced a change like the transmutation of metals. Take these as facts of sober mental history, and do they not seem to speak the presence of a supernatural Power? If the world could come to that ninth chapter of the Acts as to a modern discovery in psychology, philosophic systems would grow out of it; all futile in explanation, of the process, but all confessing the reality and the divinity of the thing.

Yet this passage in the life of one soul is a representative of a class of changes of religious character, in which it is unphilosophical not to see the working of Divine power within the enclosure of finite being. Such a passage in the life of a soul was the conversion of Luther. Such also

was that of John Bunyan and of Gilbert Tennent. Such was that of the
late Rev. Dr. Wilson of Philadelphia, who was suddenly prostrated under
conviction of sin, through a sense of the Divine goodness in the failure
of his pistol to fell his antagonist in an assault. The mental experiences
of such men, considered merely as data of mental science, deserve a con-
sideration which they do not often receive. The world, from the beginning until now, has inferred the presence of supernal agencies in the
mental changes of men, from less conclusive evidence than those fur-
nished by such conversions as these. Socrates believed—and philosophy
has revered him for the faith — that an invisible Spirit swayed his
thought, and he believed it on less evidence than this. Napoleon believed
—and poetry has discovered piety in the faith—that supernatural power
intervened in his destiny; and he believed it on less evidence than this.
It has passed into the cant of literature to ascribe inspiration, even divinity, to great minds on infinitely less evidence than this.

So have we seen and heard in our own day, and among men and
women whose names will never be heralded in biographies, evidence of
a power working in their souls, which suggests to us irresistibly the presence of God. We have seen great suddenness of conviction, — a blas-
phemer has been struck down by a sense of guilt, as if by a bolt of fire,
like that which fell at Luther's feet. We have known a velocity of move-
ment from conviction to penitence which has seemed like the speed of
light. We have learned that such processes of conviction and conversion
have tallied with the pleadings of intercessory prayer. Prayer has seemed
to be prescient of history. We must abandon the laws of natural association if, with the scriptural doctrine of regeneration in the background,
we do not see in such changes a work of God. It is not seldom that unbelief is awed into silence by them, even when they are still distasteful to
its culture. The belief is thrust upon the incredulous observer,—he cannot resist it: — "This is not the work of man; this is not hypocrisy; it is
not enthusiasm; it is no fiction of a mind fuming with effervescent sympathy; it is no nightmare of one frantic through fear of death: this is a
work of God; I can no more question it than I can question the power of
a Creator, if I see the solid globe quivering and gaping in the throes of
an earthquake."

God Is Sometimes Suggested by the Magnitude of Conversion

John Foster has observed the evidence of Almighty Power in the awakening of intellect in those who are converted in gross ignorance. He says: "It is striking to observe how the rigid soul seems to soften and grow warm, and expand and quiver with life. With the new energy infused, it struggles to work itself into freedom from the wretched contortion in which it has so long been fixed, as by the spell of some infernal magic. It is filled with a distressed and indignant emotion at its own ignorance; actuated with a restless earnestness to be informed; acquiring an unwonted pliancy of its faculties to thought. We have known instances in which the intellectual change has been so conspicuous, that even an infidel observer must have forfeited all claim to be a man of sense if he would not acknowledge: 'This, which you call divine grace, whatever it really be, is the strangest awakener of faculties, after all.'"

But what is such intellectual awakening in comparison with the moral regeneration which underlies it! When a man who has spent half a lifetime in the dens of vice comes forth to sit as a meek disciple at the Lord's table; when it is said of a scoffer, "Behold he prayeth"; when we hear a thief crying "Lord remember me"; when a man whose name has been the synonym of vileness, and whose brutality cities have borne as a curse upon their youth, becomes a preacher of Christ; when one whom the moral sense of the world has doomed as an outcast, "lost" as no other sinner on earth can be, from whom the virtuous have turned aside in the street lest they should but touch the hem of her garment, — when such a one is seen coming to Jesus, and standing behind him at his feet, weeping, and bathing them with her tears and wiping them with the hair of her head, till he who knew no sin turns and says, "Her sins, which are many, are forgiven, for she loved much," — how is it possible not to discern that God who does wonders?

Those early Christians of Rome and Corinth, — had they no evidence of God's power in regeneration, when an apostle enumerated to them the loathsome catalogue of crimes by which Paganism had degraded humanity, and then added, "such also were some of you." Had such a man as Augustine no reason for the faith which was in him, that his "evil and abominable youth," as he affirms, was transformed by "thy grace only, O Lord, thy grace only"? Was this a visionary faith to such a man as Colonel James Gardiner? Who shall say that John Newton took the name of God in vain, in ascribing to Divine power that change in his heart

which took him from the helm of a slave-ship, and taught him to com-
pose, for all succeeding ages, such a hymn as that commencing "One
there is above all others"? Had a man with such a history no right to
speak from his own experience of God's power in his soul, when he
taught us to sing:

> "Sweet was the time when first I felt
>   The Saviour's pardoning blood"?

Had he no right to sing as he did, —

> "Amazing grace, — how sweet the sound! —
>   That saved a wretch like me!"

God Is Suggested by the Phenomena of Revivals

Still another form of this illustrative evidence of Divine agency in
regeneration appears in its diffusiveness to large numbers simulta-
neously. Scarcely can a more memorable exhibition of God be found than
that presented by a revival of religion. Historians seldom take note of so
obscure an event; yet if the secret connections of revivals with the destiny
of nations could be disclosed, they would appear to be more critical
evolutions of history than the Gothic invasions. A volume has been compiled, narrating the decisive battles of the world. But more significant
than this, and probing deeper the Divine government of the world, would
be the history of revivals.

Our sense of the reality of revivals as revelations of God is apt to be
impaired by several causes. In certain periods their frequency so familiar-
izes our minds with them that they impress us as little as the tides. At
other times the very vastness of their extent overpowers our ability to
associate them with definite thoughts of God. It is our weakness, that in
spiritual things our vision is often more intense in the specific and the
minute, than in the multifarious and the immeasurable, disclosures of
his working. Does not a single star in the sky sometimes move us more
sensibly than the whole spangled heavens, roofing the world over? So
the conversion of one soul may seem to bring us nearer to the Infinite
Mind than days of Pentecost. Perhaps, more than all else, the pathological infirmities and the moral perversions, with which human nature
defaces God's work in wide-spread revivals, fascinate our gaze as we look
on. Our vision grows distorted. We cease to discern between good and

evil. We become like men who are color-blind. We are unconscious that it is our own disease which dims our eye.

But to any sane mind whose vision faith has sharpened, so that it can see truth luminous through murky surroundings, a revival of religion will appear to be one of the most godlike events in history. Regarded as an achievement of power only, to be made the theme of philosophical inquiry, it can be traced to no human forces.

Viewed as an index of prophecy, it is often one of the night-signals of this world's march heavenward.

That swaying of a nation to and fro by secret agency, — by a Power which no man sees, and no man hears, and no man can explain; of which no man can tell whence it comes or whither it goes, yet a Power which every man feels; and which singles out from the innumerable throng this one and that one, by laws of selection which no man can define, till scores grow to hundreds, and hundreds to thousands, and an army of the elect gathers at the bidding of this voiceless One, — what mystery of faith could invite such incredulity as that involved in denying to such a phenomenon the will of God? If men would but apply to the history of revivals the same laws of cause and effect which they adopt in reasoning upon the origin of the Crusades, no man, with the scriptural idea of regeneration as a hypothesis in his mind, could withstand the evidence of Almighty Power in any revival which has commanded the faith of the church as a work of the Holy Ghost. We may sum up the testimony of such revivals, taken in the mass with all their perversions, in the confession made by many irreligious men of the last century, who had lived through the "Great Awakening" of that period, and by many also who have recently watched the phenomena of the "Year of Grace" in Ireland, that the events of which they had been eyewitnesses were inexplicable by any psychological laws which should not recognize the presence and the direct working of God in the souls of men.

God Is Suggested by Unconscious Conversion
A certain class of facts, which indeed are exceptional in their character, are yet among the signal exhibitions of God in Christian experience. I allude to certain abnormal growths of Christian life which are unproductive of Christian joy. To those who are familiar, to any large extent, with unwritten Christian biography, this will suggest a distinct and most instructive class of examples of regenerate experience. They utter

unconscious testimony to the working of Him whose glory it is to conceal a thing. When certain varieties of temperament come under the sway of regenerating grace they shrink instinctively from faith, even from hope, that the life of God may have been imparted to such as they. The credibility of experience in these cases is marred by no overweening self-confidence. The most fastidious sceptic is not here repelled by the assumptions of haughty sanctity. No honest lip can curl in contempt of the inconsistency of character with profession. These Christians make no professions. They express no assurance. They enjoy little or no hope for themselves. The inner life of some of them is as the valley of the shadow of death. Yet who that knows anything of unrecorded Christian history does not recall some from this group of crushed spirits, who have exhibited to all spectators an overwhelming testimony to the working within them of Infinite Power? They have seemed to exhale the evidence of God's indwelling. They have commanded from others a confidence which they dared not whisper to themselves. They have been as unconscious as infancy of the beauty of the Divine life they expressed. They know not that their faces shone. Men stand in awe of such characters, and gather around them to make obeisance to them. God has indeed chosen these weak things to confound the wise. Sceptics are dumb in their presence; rude men are mellowed; and strong men bow themselves at the glance of their meek eye. They make us weep when they speak of God's dealings with them. Their silence is more eloquent than speech. "I saw under the altar the souls of them that were slain for the word of God, and for the testimony which they held." In emergencies of our mental life do we not sometimes turn to these voiceless witnesses for refuge? Does not our coarser faith lean upon them with a firmer trust than upon, strong men armed, and mighty men of valor? We are not careful at such times to inquire whether the emotions which overwhelm us can be justified by this world's wisdom. We do not care whether they can be accounted for by a syllogism. Something within us assures us that in communing with such beings we hold converse with Him whose temple they are. We bid kings and counsellors of the earth to fall back to the right and the left, and let these few choice spirits go up before us. We follow those who have been chosen kings and priests unto God.

This unconscious testimony to the Divine indwelling occasionally exhibits itself in strange—yes, in fearful—forms; for it is contrasted with strange and fearful forms of suffering. I can never listen to the singing of some of the hymns of Cowper, without a thrill of reverence for the grace of God which could work so mightily in a diseased soul. Some of Cowper's most affecting lyrics, to which millions of Christian hearts have turned lovingly, as to the most truthful expression of their own experience which they have ever found, except in the Psalms of David, were composed during those eleven years in which, as he tells us, not a solitary moment of hope of his own salvation ever cheered his soul. By those rivers of Babylon he sat down and wept; and his wailings are heard in thousands of the sanctuaries of Zion to this day. Oh, mystery of grace, — that regenerating love should thus gleam out, and make radiant the path of sympathizing beholders, when not a ray of it could find ingress to the bleared and swollen eye of the unconscious believer!

May we venture to probe the mystery? Can it be the object of such a phenomenon to give to the universe a monument of God's triumph over Satan, in a conflict the severity of which *submerges* weak human nature to depths which light cannot pierce? In the shock and struggle of that warfare, in which the supremacy over man's soul is contested by unseen belligerents, may it not be that God sometimes suspends the hiding of his power, and lays out the forces of his will in majesty which the human consciousness cannot bear to look upon? Shall man see God in such conflicts and live? But the reflex influence of such experience upon the usefulness of the believer is more intelligible. I have heard it said by one, the fragrance of whose memory yet fills our New England churches, that "no man could be qualified to write a commentary on the Psalms of David who had not known some great sorrow." So, when God regenerates a chosen one who is to become dear to the hearts of many generations, the secret method of grace sometimes is to work out the change by processes which shall disclose its reality to all minds but his. To him the volume is sealed until the time of the end. Yet his tremulous fingers have written it that the Scriptures might be fulfilled: "I will lead the blind by a way they knew not; I have surnamed thee, though thou hast not known me."

Even upon the insane experience of such a soul we may reasonably found our faith in the divinity of the Power which dwells in it. We turn from the testimony of such a one in his despair, to his testimony as we doubt not he rehearses it to awe-struck angels. "Poor Cowper," as thy

friends used to call thee, "our guide, our teacher, our brother," rather
would we name thee,—what thinkest thou now of God's dealings with
thy soul? Dost thou not now understand those mysterious eleven years?
Was it not worth eleven years of sorrow to be thus enabled to express
some of the experiences of God's people in all coming time? Was it not
worth eleven years of conflict to be thus disciplined as the witness of God
to unborn millions among whom this shall be told as a memorial of thee?
Was it not worth eleven years of bondage to the powers of darkness to
be thus led to the composition of one such song of Zion as that in which
thou bast taught us that "God moves in a mysterious way"? Was it not
worth eleven years of despair to be thus moved by the throes of thine
own anguish to assure all other believers, as thou bast done, that "There
is a fountain filled with blood"? Dost thou not now see that when thou
didst say for our comfort:

> "Then, in a nobler, sweeter song,
>   I'll sing thy power to save,"

thou didst speak words of unconscious prophecy?

V. DOCTRINE OF SUPERNATURAL REGENERATION

The doctrine of Divine agency in regeneration is fruitful of practical
results. Of these one of the most obvious is a disclosure of

The Profound Nature of Depravity

Evil is radically crafty. The serpent was more subtle than any beast of
the field. We get even from an experience of sin no such profound notion
of it, as we derive from the means and powers necessary to eradicate it.
So we approximate the radical idea of depravity most nearly, through
this revelation of God's work in the new birth.

To discern the vital truth here, unconfounded by fictitious alleviations,
we need to guard our thoughts against the conception of a depravity
which is not guilt. In the subject of a moral government guilt and depravity are equivalents.

Depravity, as has been shown in a previous chapter, in any sense of
it which makes it an object of moral displeasure, is character; nothing
less, nothing more. And depraved character is guilt. The need of a work

of God to change the heart suggests, therefore, the depth of this depravity of character which the common sense of men recognizes, and the common conscience condemns as guilt. The necessity in question is proof of the exceeding sinfulness of sin. It denounces no involuntary corruption; it permits no such burial of our sense of personality. It demands no conviction of sin for constitutional degeneracy; it inflicts no such suffocation upon conscience. The soul that sinneth, it shall die. The son shall not bear the iniquity of the father.

The necessity of creating extinguished faculties would be a light matter in comparison with that which actually presses upon an unregenerate soul. The real emergency of the case probes deeper. It reaches down, down, to the lowest depths of conscience, where such ideas as right, wrong, guilt, remorse, punishment, pardon, are the elements; down below theories of the make of the soul as a creature of power, below the stock it comes from as a prisoner of the body; down to what the soul is in its own chosen being. And there, in that underground of conscious character, regenerating love finds faculties not one of which is defunct, sensibilities which are all quivering with life, a will which baffles death in its tenacity; an unshattered soul, which in its wholeness can obey God, and will not. The sinner can give to God *all there is of him*—and will give nothing. The depravity therefore which his dependence proves, I repeat, is the depravity of guilt. Such depravity is an incomparably more fearful thing, for it is more profound and more hateful, than degeneracy of stock or taint in the blood. The difference is the measureless one between misfortune and crime. Morally estimated, the misfortune is nothing— the crime infinite. The degeneracy of blood is only a condition of probation—the depravity of guilt is a chosen doom.

What, then, must such depravity be, if it be so profound as to need the intervention of Omnipotence to root it out? Divest the thought for a moment of technical dialect. Conceive what must be the character of that intelligent soul, that sane mind, that free being, that responsible man, whose sheer guilt constitutes his helplessness, and creates his need of the interposition of a power such as has no parallel that we know of in God's working elsewhere. Who shall gauge that moral abyss in which a soul lies, when, with its godlike endowments of intelligence, conscience, and freedom intact, it is fallen because it would plunge down; prostrate, because it will not rise; guilty, because the unmitigated and unrelenting forces of its will are concentrated in the choice to be so; and therefore its salvation is thrown back—an anomaly in the history of the universe —upon the resources of Infinite Mind? By what similitude shall we paint such a being's unlikeness to God? What shall we call him? Yet such is man as the gospel finds him. Such is man lost, the world over. Such is man unregenerate in schools of science and in homes of refinement, as well as in the abodes of poverty and the lairs of vice. To the dispassionate thoughts of God this ruin of soul is a reality, whatever we may think of it. His calm eye looks down on the stream of busy life that flows through our streets, and singles out this lost one and that lost one—how many, who dares to conjecture?—"Lord, is it I?" To him this desolation of godlike being is a reality as vivid as the great white throne.

The moral uses of this doctrine of the New Birth disclose also with singular beauty

The Harmony of Truth with the Nature of Mind

No other theory of human nature prostrates man so low before God; yet no other uses so honestly for the purpose of that abasement man's own intelligence, the workings of his own reason, the longings of his own heart, the convictions of his own conscience. Confronted with the Word of God on this subject, a man is made to see with his own eyes, to hear with his own ears, to understand with his own intellect, to interpret his own nature, to feel in his own consciousness, and, if regenerated, to yield in his own personality. Thus, the whole man is humbled. No one part of him gives the lie to another. God's work within him does not falsify his necessary beliefs. He is not made a maniac or a fanatic or a mystic. Nor is he left for one moment to the reasonable indulgence of a conception which jars the integrity of his conscience, or taints with suspicion his thoughts of God. Truth here, as in all other revelations of itself, hints at a system of congruities.

Through this opening we have also an impressive outlook upon

Man's Renewal as a Work Worthy of God

One of the most suggestive thoughts in our modern literature is the title of a sermon by one of our own preachers: "The Dignity of Human Nature shown from its Ruins." So we might discourse of the "Majesty of God as shown in the Reconstruction of the Ruins of the Fall." In this work God does but reclaim his own. He rebuilds the fragments of his own image. His work is the more godlike, the more loftily we exalt the human constitution within which he operates. In this we indulge no self-assertion: we only assert God. For, the more godlike the man in his endowments as regenerating grace finds him, the more awful has been the shock of his fall, the more profound is the depth of his ruin, and the more superhuman, therefore, are the attributes exhibited in his recovery. We have no pinions with which to wing our flight to the altitude of such an achievement. We can only look on speechlessly at a work so much like God in its conception, and so honorable to him in its consummation.

The Lowliness of God

Yet we change our position by a step only, and we see not so much the sovereignty as the condescension of God in the New Birth.

It is characteristic of those aspects of truth which from one angle of vision display the Divine dignity most impressively, that from another they exhibit the Divine lowliness inexplicably. So it is with the work of God in man's renewal. Viewed from above as a work of dominion, nothing appears more like a Sovereign God; yet, viewed from within, nothing seems its equal as a disclosure of a condescending and self-forgetful Friend.

Said Whitefield, on one occasion when overcome by a sense of his personal election by the Divine mercy: "Why me, Lord; why me?" So might we inquire respecting every renewed child of Adam: Why has God chosen this one? Why that one? Why is a fallen one singled out from this boundless universe of souls? Why should God stoop and reach down so low? Why expend his wisdom, his power, his patience, his love, his complicated and costly beneficence, on passions so odious and hearts so obdurate? We can have no adequate conception how odious they are to him. We, through mere refinement of taste, revolt from contact with guilt in its grosser forms. When a sensitive woman encounters savage vices to save the souls of men, we look on with awe. But few understand the sacrifice. We call it a heroism which is not of this world. Yet what, in the comparison, must every unrenewed heart be to the mind of God, — a Mind infinite in its sensibilities as well as in its perceptions; a Mind, therefore, whose recoil from sin is an unrevealed experience, because no other mind is capable of conceiving such a revelation? It should not have surprised us if God had deemed it beneath his dignity to regenerate a depraved soul. So man would have reasoned. We should have said that

Divine magnanimity ought not to be thus humiliated. Omniscient thought ought not to be abased, immaculate purity ought not to be contaminated, infinite love ought not to be shocked, the eternal choice ought not to be degraded by such inglorious association. Why did not God reason so? Why did he not simply doom the ruin to its desolation? Why did he not bury its ghastliness from the sight of the universe, and leave it there?

The Holy Spirit is a Personal Friend

This subject also individualizes the Holy Spirit as a personal Friend. That is not an unmeaning peculiarity of the plan of salvation which assigns to the distinctions in the Godhead diverse relations to this work. A mature Christian experience finds no unnaturalness in a concentration of itself at times upon one or another of these manifestations of God in redemption. That is an imperfect acquaintance with God which has not led the heart to embrace, in its distinct consciousness of affection, the Holy Ghost. Our Saviour knew the cravings of the regenerate heart when he gave to the Holy Spirit a sympathetic rather than a reverend title: "The Comforter, he dwelleth with you." Christian life expresses one of its most profound realities in that language of affectionate praise in which psalmists have taught us to address the third person of the Trinity.

> Lord, am I precious in thy sight?
>   Lord, wouldst thou have me thine?
> May it be given me to delight
>   The Majesty divine?
> O Holy Spirit! dost thou mourn
>   When I from thee depart?
> Dost thou rejoice when I return,
>   And give thee back my heart?
>
> O happy Heaven! where thine embrace
>   I never more shall leave,
> Nor ever cast away thy grace,
>   Nor once thy Spirit grieve.

The Law of Dependence

We may learn, finally, from this theme one element of the spirit with which men should seek their own salvation. No sinner can seek eternal life aright, none will seek it in earnest, whose soul is not pervaded with the conviction of his need of a change which must be wrought by the power of the Holy Ghost. The soul must again stand face to face with God, as in the hour of its creation. This conviction cannot legitimately lead to helpless inactivity. It cannot tempt to impenitent delay of duty. The sense of moral helplessness is never to be sought as an end; it is to be used as a means. Its proper drift is to deepen more profoundly the sense of guilt, until the sense of guilt shall impel the sinner to Him who only can redeem. This, then, is the conviction which should be impressed upon an unregenerate sinner. He should feel that he is so overloaded by his own sins, he is so obstinate in his own perverseness, he is so prostrate in the helplessness of his own guilt and in the guilt of his own helplessness, that nothing but Almighty Grace will save him. This is the measure of his guilt, — that he needs Omnipotence to change his heart. No other view than this meets the facts of a sinner's condition. He is thus in the hands of God. He is thus dependent on God's will for his conversion. He is made thus dependent by his own wilfulness in sin; by nothing else. This is dependence in the supreme degree. It is ultimate, as no other dependence can be.

The question of a sinner's salvation, therefore, must be suspended upon God's own good pleasure. It is no anomaly that the result is locked up in the recesses of an eternal purpose. It is no merciless decree that he hath mercy on whom he will have mercy. It is in love that the sinner is permitted to stand in this emergency alone with God. It is the joy of Christian faith to leave him there. The solicitude of friends must leave him there. All human appliances and means of grace must leave him there, — in the hands of God. We entertain no views of truth which would remove him from those everlasting arms. We teach no such theology as would relieve him from this dependence of guilt upon Almighty Grace. We can gather around him, with our solicitudes, instructions, persuasions, entreaties, warnings. We can go with him to the throne of mercy, and there plead for him. But there our work ceases. We must, and we rejoice that we may, leave him there, — each one, shut into his own solitude with God.

Chapter 3

Truth: The Instrument of Regeneration

It is the misfortune of some of the doctrines of our religion that theological inquiry has often confounded their speculative with their practical elements. Questions respecting them which never can be answered in this world have stood side by side, as if of equal moment, with those which must be answered if an earnest mind would find peace. The views of truth which are commended to the faith of an inquirer often exhibit, therefore, a singular medley of knowledge and conjecture. Volumes have been compiled of the Curiosities of Literature. A good service would be rendered to practical religion if the curiosities of theology could be detached from its essential facts, yet without abridgment of legitimate theological inquiry.

The necessity of such a distinction becomes the more obvious the nearer we approach to any one of those centres of theological thought which represent an intermingling of agencies in human destiny. Such a centre of truth is the doctrine of The New Birth. In the spirit of these remarks, let us now consider the *Instrumentality of Truth in Regeneration*.

I. BIBLICAL VIEW OF TRUTH AS A POWER

The scriptural representations on this subject are not recondite; yet they cover all these points of inquiry on which we need instruction, that we may form a consistent theory of the working of Divine Grace. They may be cited, not so much for their force as proof-texts, as for their pertinence in giving us the inspired doctrine in inspired expression. Fortunately, the most salient of the passages declarative of this doctrine need no comment. To utter them is to explain them. It is difficult to mistake the import of the text: "Of his own will begat He us with the word of truth." To the same effect is the Psalmist's declaration: "The law of the Lord is perfect, converting the soul." The entire burden of the one hundred and nineteenth Psalm is a tribute of adoration to Truth as an instrument of Divine purposes. Why was Paul "not ashamed of the gospel of Christ"? Because "it is the power of God unto salvation."

Dogmatic statements of doctrine, however, are not the favorite forms of inspiration. The most emphatic representations of doctrine in the Scriptures are pictures. Their forces of expression depend on the significance of figurative language. Scriptural style is thus hieroglyphic. "I have heard of Thee," one might say, in comparing the biblical revelation of God with uninspired theology, "I have heard of Thee by the hearing of the ear, but now mine eye seeth Thee." We must, therefore, often interpret calm and literal declarations by the light of other texts, in which the same truths are more intensely expressed or implied in metaphor. We must gain vividness of impression at the expense of literal accuracy of formula.

Thus Truth, as an instrument of God's will, is at one time a lamp to the feet of a wanderer; it is a light shining in a dark place. Then it is a voice from heaven; it crieth at the gates of cities; it is more, it is the rod of God's mouth; yet it is songs in a pilgrimage. Again, it is an incorruptible seed; seed sown in good ground; it is an engrafted word. Martial images and mechanic powers and the elements of nature are laid under tribute to express it. It is a sword, the sword of the Spirit, sharper than any two-edged sword; it is a bow made naked; the wicked are slain by it. It is a helmet, a shield, a buckler; it is exceeding broad; it cannot be broken. Goads, nails, fire, a hammer, are its symbols. It breaketh the flinty rock; it is mighty to the pulling bows of strongholds. Opposite and contrasted emblems are tasked to portray its many-sided excellence. It is a fountain; it runneth very swiftly: yet it standeth forever; it is settled in heaven; it cannot be moved till heaven and earth pass away. It is of ancient birth; before the mountains were settled, it was brought forth; when there were no fountains it was there. The choicest and most fascinating objects of man's desire are the imagery of its magnificence. It is a revenue, better than choice silver; men shall, buy and sell not again; happy is the man that findeth it. It is a pearl of great price; better than rubies; like apples of gold; yet to him that thirsteth, it is wine and milk, which, in the affluence of the supply, shall be given away without money and without price. The senses of the body and its most necessary functions are made to set forth the efficacy of truth. Men taste it as a luscious food; it is sweet to the taste; sweeter than the honeycomb. Their hands have handled it, as a work of rarest art. They have walked in it, as in a path at noonday. Yet they have hidden it in their hearts; and there it quickeneth, it strengtheneth; it hath made men free; it giveth life; men are born again by the Word. Even the most daring mysteries of speech are resorted to, to intensify truth as a power in the universe. It dwelt with God. Before the hills, and when there were no depths, then was it by him, as one brought up with him; it rejoiced, always before him. And more, it is God: "I am the Truth;" again, it is God: "the Spirit is Truth."

By such versatility and boldness of imagery do the sacred writers pour out in profusion their conceptions of truth as an instrument in the execution of God's will. And it is by the aid of these picturesque Scriptures that we must vivify our interpretation of those declarative passages which express logically the instrumentality of truth in regeneration.

It is very obvious that the inspired writers have not thought it essential to the objects of their mission to measure and weigh their words, to meet exigencies suggested by metaphysical inquiry. They have spoken as freely, as boldly, with as spontaneous and unguarded speech, on this subject, as on that of the holiness or the love of God. Theirs is the dialect of song, rather than of diplomacy. They have spoken as if they were not thinking of any philosophy to be defended or destroyed, or of any polemic strategy to be executed or evaded, by the doctrine they should teach. They have spoken like plain men talking to plain men. They have uttered truth vividly rather than warily. They evidently trusted much for the correct interpretation of their language to the common sense of their readers. They have assumed many things, they have omitted to guard against many misconstructions, because of their confidence in common sense. The necessary beliefs of the race, of which common sense is the exponent, lie back of inspired language, as of all language.

We must bear this in mind in any attempt to reduce the scriptural declarations to the formulary of a creed. With this precaution, we may safely infer from them all that we need to know respecting both the fact and the mode of the action of truth in regeneration.

II. INSTRUMENTALITY OF TRUTH A FACT IN REGENERATION

It is scarcely possible to reverent inquiry to err on this point. This is an elemental fact in scriptural theology, which no necessities of philoso-phy should tempt us to fritter away. Specifications of it may be concisely stated in the following form:

First, that God employs in regeneration Truth as distinct from instru-ments of physical power. God is wisely studious of congruities. He adapts the instrument to the effect. He selects that which in its nature is fitted to act upon mind, not upon matter. He chooses that which is pre-ad-justed to the regeneration of mind, not to its creation. He calls to his ser-vice that which intelligence can perceive, heart can feel, will can choose; that which, therefore, the whole man can accept, trust, love, obey.

Again, God employs in regeneration Truth as distinct from falsehood. Not a shadow of evidence appears in the Scriptures that a human heart was ever changed from sin to holiness by the force of error. No man was ever moved aright by wrong. No soul ever thrived upon lies. Profound and honest belief of the false can never, in its own proper drift, save a man. If it seems to save, there is a way that seems right, but the ends thereof are the ways of death. If the man is saved in his error, he is not saved by it, but by truth lodged somewhere in it. Pure error tends to de-struction as inevitably as fire. An echo comes down the ages of inspira-tion, "that they all might be damned who believe not the truth."

Furthermore, God employs in regeneration religious Truth as distinct from all other truth. Not the axioms of mathematics, which appeal only to man's sense of the true; not truths which address only man's sense of the beautiful; not truths which move only man's sense of grandeur; not truths which gratify only man's love of mystery; not truths which quicken only man's sense of honor; not truths which take possession only of man's social affections; not these are the causal instrument of the new birth. Right, holiness, law, love, God, — such are the rudimentary ideas of truth in this divine renewal. Primarily and ultimately they appeal to conscience. Through this regal faculty they command the whole soul.

Moreover, in the regeneration of those to whom the Christian revela-tion is given, God employs as his chosen and final instrument, Truth as it radiates from the person and the work of Christ: "I am the Truth; I am the Life;" "The Gospel of Christ is the power of God unto salvation"; "Nothing, save Jesus Christ and Him crucified."

The Instrumentality of Truth Invariable

Yet once more, so far as we can know, God never dispenses with the agency of Truth in renewing the hearts of men. If a question be raised here, it should concern, not the power of God, but the facts of his working. So far as any essential doctrine of theology is concerned, it may or may not be true that infinite power can regenerate a soul by other instrumentalities, or without the intervention of instrument. For the purposes of a practical faith, it may or may not be true that, in the nature of things, regeneration is an act which, apart from the instrumentality of truth, sustains no relation even to omnipotence. Be it so, or be it not, that to the Divine Mind truth and regeneration — the instrument and the effect — stand in relations of necessity immutable and eternal, like the laws of numbers or of diagrams, we need not affirm or deny. The theological question, if any exists, is a simple question of fact. Does God in the renewal of a human soul ever dispense with truth as the instrument of the change?

The answer to this question is not wholly unimportant to consistency of faith. It can be given in few words. It is comprised in two positions, which a moment's reflection will establish.

One is, that if God does in any instance dispense with truth as his moral instrument in the new birth, the evidence of this fact must be a subject of pure revelation. Experience, from the nature of the case, cannot prove it. No man can intelligently affirm himself to be conscious of a divine fiat thrilling his nature, making a new man of him, with no instrumental agency, or with other instrumentality than that of truth. The only evidence any man can have from experience that his heart is changed is the evidence of actual exercises of heart in view of truth. Divine power in the change is, to all consciousness, so blended with the force of truth, — in other words, the efficient cause so interpenetrates the instrumental cause, — that no mind can intelligently separate them. Indeed, consciousness gives us no hint of the Divine Cause, except through the success of the instrument. I cannot go back of my own conscious exercises in view of truth, and affirm that God has changed my heart by sheer will, independently of truth. It is plainly impossible; as absolutely so as that my eye should detect the undulations of sound, or my ear those of light. Regeneration, the divine act, is evidenced to consciousness only by conversion, the human change; and this, again, discloses itself only in responses of the soul to truth. Experience can go no further back than this; and if experience cannot, observation cannot. If, then, God has ever wrought the renewal of a soul in such anomalous manner as that implied in the inquiry before us, the evidence of the fact must be a subject of direct and supernatural revelation; we can know it only from the Scriptures.

The second position, then, in answer to this inquiry, is, that the Scriptures are silent as to the occurrence of any such instance in the history of redemption. They do not explicitly deny, but neither do they affirm. They inform us of many instances of regeneration by means of truth; and of not one without the truth. They proclaim indubitably the law of divine working in this, phenomenon of human experience; and they neither by assertion nor hint point us to a solitary exception. They record none in the world's history; they predict none in its future. Here, therefore, argument on this topic may legitimately end. In all our positive reasonings upon it we must assume that no such exception exists. In our practical uses of the doctrine we must assume that none will exist to the end of time. We cannot logically found any article of our faith on the hypothetical possibility that the fact is otherwise.

The Regeneration of Infants

But if conjecture, wiser than truth, must still press inquiry and ask: "How are infants regenerated who die before moral responsibility commences?" we respond by inquiries which are at least as wise; though for ourselves we do not revere them, nor are our dreams troubled if we cannot answer them. We respond by asking: How do you know that they are regenerated? How do you know that irresponsible beings are proper subjects of "regeneration" in the sense in which the Scriptures apply the word to adult sinners? Who has told you that the new birth has any relation to irresponsible infancy more than to irresponsible idiocy? Is a change of heart conceivable in a being who has no heart? What is regeneration in an irresponsible soul? What authority have we for believing anything of such a nondescript? Shall the whole drift of the Scriptures be held in check by conjectural philosophy?

But, again, how do you know that there are any such infants? Where is it revealed that a soul has ever left this world, or ever will, with moral nature absolutely undeveloped? Who can assure you that moral birth and physical birth are not simultaneous? Who can prove that because a being cannot discern between its right hand and its left, therefore it cannot in any respect or in any degree distinguish right *thought* from wrong? How much do we know of the possibilities of infantile intuitions? Besides, who knows what the process of dying is, as a means of moral development? Have we never seen an aged infant in its coffin? Moreover, is not the death of an infant, itself an abnormal event? May it not then be one of a group of anomalies which involve an anomalous probation and an anomalous qualification for heaven?

Yet once more: if infants are proper subjects of the same change which adults undergo in regeneration, then are they not sinners? If sinners, have they not sinned? If they have sinned, can they not repent? If they can either sin or repent, can they not know right and wrong; therefore may not they too, in a future world, declare gratefully: "Of his own will begat He us with the word of truth"? Have ye not read: Out of the mouth of babes and sucklings thou hast perfected praise? Who shall dare to limit God's power of converse with the tiniest image of his own being? Are not the whole heavens mirrored in the retina of a single eyeball? How much greater is the distance—and what matters it to his resources —between God and a speechless babe than between God and you or me? How do we know that in the world of infantile seclusion, before speech has broken the eternal silence from which that world has sprung, God has not ordained a system of moral correspondences with heaven, on which he administers a government of freedom, of law, and of brace, as perfect in its kind as that of Eden; a system which he guards as lovingly as ours; and a system before the mysteries of which angelic wisdom bends reverently, as we stand in awe around the marvels of the microscope? Is such a system any more incomprehensible or incredible than the laws of communication by instinct in humming-birds? Is it any more marvellous than the autocracy of a beehive?

We confess to an aesthetic sympathy with Wordsworth's fancy in the following lines:

> "Thou who didst wrap the cloud
> Of infancy around us, that Thyself
> Therein with our simplicity awhile
> Mightest hold on earth communion undisturbed."

Theologically, we see no absurdity in the hope that this may be more than poetry. Yet we cannot fortify the hope by revelation or by reason.

The proof-texts—where are they? The logic of the facts—to whom has infantile experience disclosed it? Our memory is very reticent; our observation is very ignorant. To our reason, "the cloud of infancy" is very dense. To our faith, the Bible is very still. What moral mysteries are latent in infantile mind we therefore do not affirm or deny. We do not know. If revelation had been addressed to infants it might have made us more knowing than we are; but, alas, we cannot be wise above that which is written for our admonition. Yet, if the Scriptures had answered the "obstinate questionings" of wise men on this theme, could the world have contained the books which should be written.

III. The Mode in Which Truth Acts in Regeneration

Assuming, then, the fact of the invariable instrumentality of Truth in regeneration so far as we know, we are prepared to observe further such intimations as the Scriptures give us respecting the mode in which Truth operates in the change.

Here, again, the Bible can scarcely be said to affirm anything except by implied assumption. One vital principle is thus affirmed. It is that of the coincidence of the operation of truth with the laws of the human mind. Truth is everywhere used in the Bible precisely as men are wont to use it in persuasive speech. There is a freedom in its use; there is a skill in its use; there is a mingling of boldness and adroitness in its use; there is a studious care to adjust it to its use; there is a wise control of it, now by utterance, now by reserve, in its use by inspired minds; and there is a confidence, yes, a triumph, in their assertions of its power, which appear to assume that truth has intrinsic fitness to move a human mind; and if to move it, to move it aright; and if to move it aright, to move it in genial consistency with its own laws.

Where do we find in the Scriptures disparagement of truth as a power over unregenerated mind? Where is the proof that the divine choice of it as an instrument was arbitrary? Where is a hint given of its being a fictitious or a factitious means to the end it is used for? Why should we search for it as for hidden treasure, if intrinsically it has no worth, or if any other instrument divinely chosen could be as worthy? That is not a salutary faith which depredates the inherent potency of truth. Divine sovereignty gains no honor, and needs none, from the reproach of its

instrument. Are God and Truth rivals in our esteem? That is not a rational fear, then, which shrinks from "means" of regeneration, and especially from "natural means." Not so do we read the Word of God. The
change from sin to holiness as portrayed in biblical speech strikes us as
a restorative, not a destructive process. It may be tumultuous, but it is
not therefore discordant with the laws of mind. Truth energized by the
Holy Spirit may take possession of a man impetuously, so that whether
he is in the body or out of the body he cannot tell; but his experience is
not therefore unnatural, or even extra-natural.

The usages of scriptural appeal are conclusive in their implications on
this topic. How do inspired men preach? They reason with men; they
invite men; they instruct men; they urge men; they entreat men; they
warn men; they rebuke men; they accumulate and reiterate all the legitimate arts of persuasion in addressing men; as if men, regenerate or
unregenerate, elect or non-elect, were proper subjects of persuasion; as
if they were complete men in their endowments; and therefore as if it
were the normal action of their being to obey the truth. The Bible assumes that man everywhere, under all conditions of probation, has intellect which can receive truth, sensibilities which can respond to truth, a
will which can act in view of truth, and act aright. So far as the philosophy of the operation of truth is concerned, we cannot see that the Scriptures make any distinction between fallen and unfallen mind. We cannot
discover that the methods of speech chosen by Isaiah, Paul, John, are not
precisely the same in addressing men before regeneration as after. What
is the difference? Where is the proof of it?

Nothing but the necessities of a philosophical theory can extract from
the Scriptures the dogma that truth is an instrument arbitrarily chosen
by divine wisdom, or chosen for unknown reasons, or chosen for no
perceptible fitness to move, and move aright, the most guilty and hopeless specimen of depraved mind. True, inspiration preserves a wise
silence, in direct instruction, on the whole subject of the philosophy of
regeneration; but its assumptions of the correspondence between truth
and mind are as unqualified as the boldest assertions could be. So versatile is its use of truth, so many-sided does truth appear in inspired forms,
so affluent in its resources, so intricate in its evolutions, yet so direct in
its aim, and so exultant in its consciousness of power, that we cannot but
infer the existence of versatile and profound susceptibilities to that power

in the soul to which it is addressed. So exquisite is the mutual adjustment of mind and truth as represented in the biblical forms of speech, that the entire science of persuasion might be illustrated by those forms; even by such as are addressed to the fallen, depraved, unregenerate, non-elect souls. The theory of all that the world has felt to be eloquent is realized in them.

From the scriptural uses of truth, therefore, we cannot but infer that in regeneration its action is perfectly normal to the soul. Truth and mind, in this divine change, come together not as metals held in a vice and riveted; they come as light and the optic nerve. Like seeks its like. Truth acts thus not by contravention, not even by suspension, of the laws of fallen mind. It acts in harmony with those laws, in obedience to those laws, by means of those laws. They are laws which no fall can dislocate. No degree of guilt can suspend them. Truth is thus God's instrument in effecting a change which it never could of itself effect; but the soul on which it operates is never in more healthy concord with its own being than when it yields itself to truth, and becomes a child of God. God thus wisely honors the laws which his wisdom ordained.

IV. THE SIMPLICITY OF REGENERATION

In the views thus far presented certain collateral principles are involved, which are of practical importance to the preaching and the hearing of the gospel.

Of these may be named, first, the simplicity of the work of God in the change of the human heart. We see in this mysterious act the same unostentatious blending of divine efficiency with instrumental agency that we see, the world over, in other departments of God's working. For the purposes essential to faith in the doctrine of the new birth, the change is as intelligible as vegetation. It is as comprehensible as the phenomenon of sleep. The change from sleep to waking is no less mysterious. The beating of your heart is no less incredible. The laws of mind are as benevolently guarded in the one case as those of vegetable and animal life in the others.

This view should specially commend itself as a corrective of certain prejudices which may be fatal to religious life. Is there not a class of solidly built minds which are nonetheless constitutionally incredulous of a supernatural regeneration, because they have no conception of it as anything else than the effect of a shock inflicted upon the spiritual nature? They imagine it as involving a suspense of conscious personality. They have heard believers affirm that it may be imparted to a man in sleep. The creation of Eve seems to them not an inapt symbol of it. Hence, they rank faith in it with other eccentricities of dreams. Their good sense revolts from the whole thing. Have we not known certain timid minds which have believed, indeed, but only to shrink from their faith as a practical experience, because their faith also is steeped in materialism? Regenerating grace as they conceive of it is spiritualized electricity. They recoil from a religious life, for a reason analogous to that which leads them to draw back from a voltaic battery. Contortions, spiritual or muscular, are alike repulsive. Some, too, believe only to despair of salvation; others, only to live in sullen impenitence, because they are not conscious of the infusion of new vitality into their moral being. Do not pastors often encounter sad inquirers, whose minds are saturated with conceptions of the new birth scarcely more spiritual than those of Nicodemus? Are not these conceptions in part the result of accepting literally the symbolic language of the pulpit in the enforcement of this doctrine? I have known a man to watch and pray for palpable concussion with the regenerating Power, as he would spread his sails to catch the winds if he were becalmed at sea. Such unfortunate experiences are the legitimate fruit of any theory of regeneration which reduces a change of heart to an infraction of nature.

But viewed as the normal effect of truth energized by the will of God, this divine renewal falls into the same plane with other phenomena in which cause and instrument work blended to one end. The greatness of the change is not violence of change. Supernaturalness of cause is not unnaturalness in effect. Deity in the power is not miracle in the result. In material nature, are not the most profound phenomena the most simple? The very mystery of their causation enhances by contrast their lucidness as facts. What is the most sublime change the physical world ever undergoes? Is it an earthquake? Is it not rather the noiseless change from night to day? The mightiest forces in the universe are silent forces. Who ever heard the budding of an oak? Who was ever deafened by the falling of the dew? Who was ever stunned by a solar eclipse? So is it with the august phenomenon of a change of heart. So far as we know, it is the most radical change a human spirit can experience. It is a revolutionary change. Disembodiment by death, morally estimated, is not so profound. Still, a change of heart is not an unnatural change. It is never miraculous. It is not necessarily convulsive. It is not necessarily even destructive of self-possession. God employs in it an instrument exquisitely adjusted to the mind of man as an intelligent and free being. Truth may act in it with an equipoise of forces as tranquil as that of gravitation in the orbits of the stars.

No, it is not of necessity a tumultuous experience to which God calls us when he invites us to be saved. By what emblem have the Scriptures expressed the person of the Holy Ghost? Is it an eagle? "And John bare record, saying, 'I saw the Spirit descending from heaven like a dove.' " "Come," is the select language of inspiration, "come, and you shall find" —what? struggle, terror, torture? No; "ye shall find peace." "Come ye," —come who? Come, ye strong, ye men of valor, ye mighty men armed, ye heroes? No; "come, ye that labor and are heavy laden; come, ye bruised reeds; come, ye broken-hearted; come, ye whose whole heart is faint; come, ye poor in spirit; come, ye blessed ones who hunger, who thirst, who mourn, who weep; come, ye old men whose strength faileth; come, ye youths who are as when a standard-bearer fainteth; come, ye daughters of my people who are girded with sackcloth; forbid not little children to come."

V. EVIDENCE INTELLIGIBLE TO COMMON SENSE

Another principle involved in the doctrine of the Instrumentality of Truth in regeneration, is that of the rational nature of all trustworthy evidence of religious character. A change of heart, from the nature of the case, must manifest itself. Regenerate character, like all other character, will act itself out. Like all other character, its evidence will be intelligible and forceful to the common sense of men.

Christianity, in this respect vindicates its superiority to other systems of religion. In its tests of character, as in its doctrines, it makes less demand on the credulity of men than is made by any other religion which this world has known—less even than is made by atheism. Monstrosities of life, as of belief, have been the invariable characteristic of infidelity whenever it has existed on a large scale. It appears to be growing more

inane and senile as the world grows older. The early paganism had
scarcely so wild a development of lunacy in religion as that which our
age witnesses in Mormonism, in Spiritualism, and in philosophic Pantheism. Beside everything that man has originated in religion, Christianity
is alone in the fidelity with which it stands by the convictions of the human conscience, and in the severity with which it applies the laws of
good sense to the judgment of character.

The vital test of what a man is, in the divine judgment of him, is truth
acting by the common laws of mind, and therefore working out effects
intelligible to common sense. Presentiments, irrational impressions,
apocryphal revelations, ridiculous prodigies, and outrages upon the
moral sense of mankind, find no place in the Christian groundwork of
experience. Marvellous excitements, as such, have no significance in the
Christian philosophy of conversion. Uncontrollable or unreasonable
excitements in religious life are no more commendable than any other
form of frenzy. The pathological phenomena sometimes witnessed in
revivals are a misfortune, perhaps a satanic infliction. The divine ideal
of regeneration provides no place for them, except as it tolerates compas-
sionately the infirmities of our nature. He remembers that we are but
flesh.

So, Christianity is silent when an adulterous generation seeks after
signs from heaven. When men hear voices in the air, and stare at visions
in the night, and read handwritings on the walls, and "seek unto them
that have familiar spirits, and unto wizards that peep and mutter," and
frame creeds out of the antics of "household gods"; the spirit of Christian
faith looks down calmly, and says: "The prophet that hath a dream, let
him tell a dream"; and their goes on its way. If a Christian believer lingers, trusting in prophets of lies, who say: "I have dreamed, I have
dreamed"; it turns and looks upon him as our Lord looked on Peter. The
tests by which it would try the spirit of a man all assume that God works
with natural means, by natural laws, and for results signalized by their
purity and their dignity. Intelligent faith in God; an honest discovery of
sin; spiritual craving of holiness; the trust of penitence in the blood of
Christ; the dependence of guilt upon the Holy Ghost; and a giving of the
whole soul in eternal consecration to God's service, and acceptance of
God's love, and joy in God's being — these are pre-eminent among the
responses which a regenerate heart makes to truth as the instrument of

the divine change within. They are intelligible responses. They are reasonable, natural, honorable responses. They constitute a new life in the soul, which honest men cannot help trusting, and wise men cannot help revering. "And God saw that it was good."

VI. CREED ESSENTIAL TO CHARACTER

A third principle inferable from the doctrine before us, is that of the importance of truthfulness in theological opinion. The new birth as represented in the Scriptures gives no support to the theory, so natural to superficial thought, that belief, as such, is of little moment in religion; that God will judge characters, and not creeds; that we shall not be held responsible for obeying another man's faith in preference to our own. On the contrary, in regeneration character and creed are indissolubly united. God's instrument in effecting the change is truth. Falsehood finds no place there. Truth in caricature finds none. The less a man believes of truth, the more distant is he from the probable range of regenerating grace. The more distorted a man's opinions are, the more fearful are his perils. The more negative his convictions become, the more faint becomes all reasonable hope that he will be saved. In terrific consistency with this principle is the scriptural representation of the most hopeless depth of sin, as that of those to whom God sends delusion, that they may believe a lie. God acts in regeneration where truth can act; not elsewhere. The mind that withholds itself from truth is withholding itself from God.

There is reason to believe respecting many constant listeners to the preaching of the gospel, that here is the exact point at which lies the chief obstacle in their way to heaven. They will not assent to certain truths, the force of which is essential to draw them within the range of God's regenerating decree. They are repelled by one truth; they are heedlessly confused by another; they are uninterested in a third; perhaps in part persuaded of many, they are advancing in consolidation of character with hearty opinions upon none. The Holy Spirit passes them by, because they will not credit his truth. They thrust the instrument of his grace from them, and he leaves them in their sins. He does not there his mighty works, because of their unbelief. That is in reality a delicate and perilous work which a man performs when he adopts his religious opinions. In that process often occurs the very crisis of his destiny. At that point in his experience may the contending forces for good and evil meet in fearful equipoise.

In this view, also, the varieties of opinion in evangelical theology are not unimportant. That theology which is most truthful, other things being equal, will be most successful in the salvation of souls. Every distortion of theological faith is perilous, we may be assured, somewhere in the progress of its history. False combinations of doctrines which isolated are true, or false isolations of doctrines which in combination are true, are obstructions to the work of God at some point in the development of their sequences. A disproportioned shading of a single doctrine will surely attract some mind, whose way to heaven it will darken. The foreshortening of a single group in the representation of scriptural theology may so impair its truthfulness of perspective, that to some soul, somewhere, at some time, in some juncture of probationary discipline, that shall seem to be a distorted theology, a caricature of theology, a hideous theology, and therefore a false theology—a theology which no amount of evidence can prove to a sane mind, and no authority can enforce upon a sound heart. That soul, such a theology—no matter what extreme of opinion it represents—may consign to perdition; yet it may be a gospel which angels have seemed to preach.

VII. CHRISTIANITY INDEPENDENT OF FINE ART

A fourth principle collateral to the doctrine we have considered is, that the life of Christian institutions is in great degree independent of the auxiliaries of Fine Art. Two theories respecting the relations of Christianity to art are affecting the taste and the practice of the Protestant Christian world. The one theory assumes that religion and art go hand in hand, and are equally interdependent. Certain imaginative minds even conceive of them as substantially identical. They are at least so far interchangeable that enthusiasm in the one slides naturally into enthusiasm in the other. Taste and conscience are indistinguishable. Beauty and God are one. Accordingly, it is believed that to secure to Christianity any high development in the life of a people, pre-eminence must be given to music, architecture, painting, and statuary. These, again, must be seconded by scenic forms of service and by priestly attire. A preacher must become as a lovely song and one that plays well upon an instrument. The simple meeting house of the fathers "should be turned end for end"; the organ should be the cynosure of attraction, and "the pulpit nothing but an organ." This theory, with variations, lies at the foundation of the popular taste of our own day for the revival of certain forms of medieval architecture in the construction of churches.

The other theory, without condemning one variety of art or another, as such, and as in some sense a handmaid of religion, still assumes that in the very nature of Christianity there lies a certain independence of all forms of art. The vital resources of religious power are not in them. Christian truth is sovereign over them. It uses them in their grand and spiritual dignity, but refuses to subject itself to their scenic and sensuous frivolities. This view is obviously sustained by the doctrine of divine instrumentality in regeneration. The gospel presents itself to men by that noble title: "The Truth as it is in Jesus." Its power lies in the clear, calm conceptions which mind forms of truth. Through truth thus received by a human spirit, God breathes regenerating efficacy, and man becomes a living soul.

We need not, therefore, throw back the support of Christianity upon the appendages of fine art. We care not to clothe our clergy in classic or sacerdotal robes. We must not burden our worship with responsive liturgies. We will not employ, or vie with, operatic troupes in our service of song. We dare not crowd our sanctuaries with the masterpieces of the studio. We cannot enjoy a dim religious light. We tire of the gorgeousness of mediaeval ornament and the cumbrousness of Gothic columns in the structure of our churches. The kaleidoscope of memorial windows does not quicken in us a devout spirit. Why should we struggle to reproduce, in place of our plain meeting-houses, the temples of Greece, or the basilicas of Rome, or the cathedrals of Central Europe? We will not abjure these resuscitations of art, except as they become substitutes of truth. But as such they minister to an imaginative, and therefore an effeminate, and at length a corrupt, religionism. We must say of them, "Let the dead bury their dead." We prefer that art should await the bidding of Christian truth to originate new forms more becoming than these to Christian maturity. Has Christian art no resources in reserve for a millennial future? Even in this work, let it be but a modest handmaid of the Christian conscience. Let it follow in the train of instrumentalities auxiliary to the gospel, as Miriam followed the ark of bulrushes in the flags by the river-side — afar off, to see what would be done unto the child; and, like the Hebrew maiden, let it be content to do humble and incidental service. Then that service shall work in with laws of invisible and eternal Providence.

We must not, we cannot, make the gospel dependent on any of these subordinate aids. Its great strength lies in God's independence of them. It leans to severity of tastes, and to simplicity of usages, and to forms of worship uncomplicated and unimposing to the senses. This it does through its awe-struck sympathy with the spirituality of God. The glory of its work on earth is, that as the Truth of God it can go anywhere in the strength of God. In Grecian temples, in Indian pagodas, in barbarian amphitheatres, in Turkish mosques, in mediaeval cathedrals; in Puritan conventicles, in Quaker meeting-houses, in floating bethels, in barns, in lumber-rooms, in log-huts; in the forests, at the sea-side, on the prairie; everywhere, it can be itself the power of God and the wisdom of God. Its preachers need not be learned in the millinery of churchly costume; nor careful to know whether vaulted roofs, or painted panels, or plain ceiling, or unhewn rafters, or green leaves, or the stars of heaven, are over their heads. If they can but speak God's truth as God bids them, it will do God's work.

VIII. THE TRUE IDEAL OF THE PULPIT

In sympathy with this view, the instrumentality of Truth in regeneration suggests the scriptural theory of preaching. In the light of this doctrine, preaching is a perfectly natural work, successful through supernatural power. Its object is to instruct men in the knowledge of truth, to impress truth on the conscience and the heart, and to win to obedience of truth the estranged human will. To these ends it is a perfectly philosophical means. Its action is normal to the constitution of the soul. Its aims and its methods commend themselves to the good sense of all candid minds. They are not philosophically different from those of honest speech in other forms. But unlike those, preaching is overshadowed, in the very conception of it, by the Divine Presence. There lies the sole hope of its success. Finite instrument in the hand of Infinite Power; Nature used by Him who made it: such is the true ideal of the pulpit.

Preaching, then, is no idle play for the amusement of idle minds. Its design is not to fascinate men by euphony of speech, to startle by oddity of conceit, or quaintness of imagery, or boisterous declamation. It is not to work upon the magnetic organism which unites body and mind, so as to excite sensibility not sustained by thought. Still less is it to soothe the religions instinct of men, while evading or stupefying those cravings which forecast eternity. A genuine preacher will engage in his work with intense intelligence of purpose. He will preach truth to the calm, sober judgment of men. He will lead men to a right life by implanting within them right convictions of truth. He will kindle their sensibilities by so presenting truth as to set their minds to thinking. Vividness of belief, depth of feeling, holiness of will, all borne up and ruled by truth,—these will be the object of a wise preacher's aim. These he will strive to weave into the homeliness of real life. He will preach to men's wants rather than their wishes. The *wholeness* of his soul in its co-working with God will revolt from making the pulpit anything less than a regenerating power.

He may, indeed he must, employ varied and skillful methods of address. Things new and old he will bring from his treasure. Acceptable words even, he will seek out diligently. No art of orator or poet or moral painter is unworthy of him. But the crowning feature of his work is, that it breathes with the singleness and the intensity of his desire to make truth reach and sway the whole being of his hearers, through time and in eternity; and with the courage of his faith that, in God's strength, and in that only, it will do this. This ardor of devotion to Truth, and to God in Truth, palpitates all through the structure of a Christian sermon. This makes preaching seem intensely alive and concrete. This sanctifies all art in the work of the pulpit. It subordinates art, and conceals it from obtrusion. The hearer sees no art; the preacher is conscious of none. Only God in Truth is felt in living presence. Such is the theory of preaching as implied in the divine instrumentality of the new birth.

This theory is specially opposed to a certain construction of discourses, some varieties of which, we have reason to fear, are craved by the popular taste of our own day, and are sometimes given from the pulpit.

"Great Sermons"

Here let us distinguish precisely the evil; for I must believe that undeserved censure has been broadcast upon both the pulpit and the popular taste by indiscriminate rebuke. That is not a healthful caution, for it is neither reasonable nor scriptural, nor true to the teachings of history, which decries the careful, the studied, the elaborate, the anxious use of what are ambiguously called "natural means" in preaching. God recognizes no other than natural means. Supernatural power, acting through natural means, is the divine ideal of successful preaching. So far as we have anything to do with it, the means are as essential as the power. Philosophically speaking, indeed, we have nothing to do with anything but the means. Prayer is but a means auxiliary to truth.

That is a perfectly legitimate taste, therefore, which demands *thought* in the pulpit, as everywhere else where mind attempts to influence mind. That would be a criminal weakness in the pulpit which should fail to meet such demand. We must commend the alertness of the popular mind which requires penetrative and suggestive preaching. Men always require this when they are in earnest. They have a right to it. We should not be fearful of "great sermons." We are in no peril of greatness above measure. It would be more becoming to our modesty to stir up each other's minds in remembrance of the evil wrought by small sermons. But the truth is that, in this work of preaching Christ, "great" and "small" are impertinent adjuncts. In such a work nothing is great but God; nothing small in his service. That is not only a hopeless, it is a positively false, policy, which, in its fear of an excess of stimulus in the pulpit, would put down the popular craving for thought, by inundating the pulpit with commonplaces whose only claim to attention is that they are true. Even that which is so severely and justly censured as "sensational preaching" is not so unworthy of respect as that preaching which popular impatience describes by the use of an old word in our English vocabulary, and calls it "humdrum."

The policy of frowning upon the zestful originality of the pulpit as an unholy thing is not the policy commended in the Scriptures; nor is it the policy which historically God has blessed. Apostles charge us: Be strong; quit you like men. The Bible itself is the most thrillingly living volume in all literature. Why do philosophers turn to it when all other wisdom is exhausted? Yet savages have wept, entranced by it, when they would play with their plumes under the reading of Pilgrim's Progress or Robinson Crusoe. The testimony of history is that in every period of religious awakening in the world the pulpit has been intellectually awake. Preaching has been thoughtful, weighty, pungent, startling, and timely; so broad awake as to impress the world as a novelty. At such times there is very little of conservative tranquillity in it. It seems rather to be turning the world upside down. It has always been thus; it always will be. Cannot the depth of revivals of religion be generally measured by the weight of the discussions in which the pulpit has pressed down truth into the popular heart?

The principle, in brief, which should decide all questions respecting the intellectuality of preaching is this: that the popular mind will always demand, and ought always to receive, so much of weighty, vigorous, penetrative, original thought as the popular conscience is sufficiently educated to appropriate; and it should receive no more.

Affectations of the Pulpit

But there is a style of preaching which is regardless of this principle, and of all others that concern the necessities of souls. I, refer to that structure of discourse, in which the sacredness of truth as the divine instrument of salvation is buried beneath the display of artistic skill. There is a mode of preaching in which a sermon becomes purely a work of art, and nothing more. This error exists in a variety of forms. Sometimes it is the art of constructing authoritative formula of theology. Doctrines are defined and defended with reference to nothing but their orthodoxy of statement, and their place in a catechism or a creed. Again, it is the art of scholastic reasoning. Argument is constructed with care for nothing but its logical rigidity—and, we may blandly add, its aridity. In other cases it is the art of transmutation of truth from the dialect of experience to the dialect of philosophy. Sermons are framed in morbid fear of cant and commonplace. Without one new thought, or new shading of an old thought, the preacher would fain lift up his weary and bewildered bearers from the language of life, that is, the language he has lived and therefore knows, to the language of the "higher thinking," whatever that may be. He preaches as if the chief end of man in the pulpit were to evade the peculiarities of Christian speech. In its best interpretation, his discourse is only an exchange of the cant of the church for the cant of the school.

In a still different form, this clerical affectation becomes the art of elegant literature. The graces of composition are elaborated with solicitude for nothing but its literary finish. They are drawn, like the lines of an engraving on a plate of steel, with fastidious and mincing art, studious only of their effect in a scene which is to be set in a gilded frame, and exhibited to connoisseurs. Application of truth is made, if it be made, to an imaginary audience or to an abstract man. It is clothed in archaic speech, which no man, woman, or child of a living audience will take to heart. An exhortation to repentance even may be so framed and uttered as to be nothing but the closing scene of a drama.

Perhaps the most vapid variety of these affectations of the pulpit is that which, for the want of a more significant name, may be termed the art of churchly etiquette. This is an inheritance from a dead age. Its chief aim is to chain the pulpit fast to its traditional dignity, to protect it from plebeian excitements, and specially to seclude it from the vulgarity of participation in the conflict of living opinions. With this ambition, the clergy assume the style of reverend fathers in God, and *talk down* to their hearers. Their dialect is that of affectionate patronage. They preach as an order of superior beings. At a sublime altitude above living humanity, they speak benignly to the condition of buried centuries. They discuss extinct species of thought. They exhort to untimely forms of virtue. They prop up decaying usages and obsolescent rites of worship. They are absorbed in the romance of priesthood. It may happen as an incident to their ministry that they tread delicately through the thoroughfare of a bloody revolution, affecting to ignore the forces which are embattled in the popular heart, and counting their mission successful if they keep the pulpit intact from the great agonies which are seething around it.

In a word, under such theories of preaching a sermon becomes a catechism, or a disquisition, or an essay, or an allegory, or a poem, or a painting, or a reverie, or an "encyclical letter," or a non-descript beneath all these, and nothing more. Preaching is literally reduced to an art, and religion is degraded to a science—reduced and degraded, not because of science and art, but because they are made nothing else than a science and an art, or are even made caricatures of both. The intense sacredness of truth as God's instrument in the quickening of dead souls, and in satisfying the cravings of their awakening, is lost out of sight in the preacher's solicitude for certain accuracies, or prettinesses, or dignities, or oddities, or distortions of artistic form.

Popular Criticism of the Pulpit

We are accustomed to condemn such preaching as defective in religious spirit. It is so. We say, in that most expressive dialect of Christian experience, that it wants "unction". It does so. We whisper that it betrays a moral delinquency in the preacher. We are right in this. But are we not often guilty of a fallacy in the commendations bestowed upon the very thing against which our religious instinct has hurled the heaviest anathema that can be uttered in criticism of the pulpit? Such preaching is often approved for its orthodoxy, for its science, for its literature, for its churchly dignity. You hear it commended as good doctrine, good philosophy, good logic, good rhetoric, good poetry, good painting, good acting, good manners, good art in all its forms, and yet you cannot feel it to be good preaching. It is fancied to be good for every purpose except that of doing good. The intellect, it is affirmed, approves it, imagination delights in it, sensibility revels in it, taste courts it, culture craves it, everything in man that is worthy of respect makes obeisance to one form or another of it, except his conscience; and this stands by as a disconsolate monarch, lamenting his impotence to put down as a sin that which by the consent of all allied powers is exalted as an accomplishment. Confusion follows, therefore, in clerical practice. False art comes to be recognized as the legitimate fruit of a sound faith, or a scholarly training, or a churchly taste in the pulpit. Yet the obstinate conviction is underlying all the while, that this does not meet the responsibilities of the pulpit, nor do its work. Thus a divorce at length comes about, in the very theory of what the pulpit should be, between the moral usefulness of preaching and all its other excellences.

To illustrate the truth of this in but a single phase of it: have we not learned to speak of a certain class of ministers in tones of compassionate criticism, in which our culture and our conscience give the lie to each other? We say of one of these brethren in Christ: "He is a useful preacher, but he is not eloquent. He is a good man; he is an earnest man; he is a devout man; but — he is not eloquent. He is a faithful pastor; he is a laborious pastor; he is a successful pastor; but — he is not eloquent. He is a truthful preacher; he is a sound preacher; he is a solemn preacher: flippant men are awed by the earnestness of his discourse; thinking men are strengthened by his faithful words; proud men sit as children at his feet; scoffers rage at his plain speech; men who rail at him are held, year after year, beneath his pulpit, as by an invisible hand; but — he is not

eloquent. Souls are converted under his timely ministration; somehow
—you cannot tell how, the wind bloweth where it listeth, but somehow
—he has the tongue of the learned; he knows how to speak a word in
season to him that is weary; the common people hear him gladly; woman
discerns of what spirit he is, and follows him, as she went early to the
sepulchre; and little children come running unto him and praying that
he will take, them in his arms and bless them; but, this man, so honored
of God; this man, so revered by ministering angels; this man, so much
like Christ; this man, we cannot, oh no, we dare not, pronounce — an
eloquent preacher!"

Never was a more egregious error committed than in this whole style
of criticism, in judgment of the pulpit. If nothing is beautiful but truth,
neither is anything respectable which is not true to God's thought. A
sermon which is only a model of orthodoxy, or of science, or of literature, or of churchly conservatism, and which shoots by or vaults over the
plain, living applications of truth as God's instrument in meeting the
actual condition of souls, has no qualities which should win for it the
respect of an earnest man. For the great uses of the pulpit it is an abor-
tion. The falseness of it to the mission of a preacher vitiates its very
virtues. Good taste condemns it as violently as conscience. All noble
culture cries out against it as sternly as the word of God. No tribunal is
more fatal to its claims than that of Christian scholarship. No voice is
more indignant in the rebuke of it than that of the most accomplished
manhood. Such preaching is not only not good preaching, but it is not
anything else which a symmetrical and earnest soul can approve.
Demosthenes, Chatham, John Adams, had they been preachers of the
gospel, would never have preached thus, any more than Paul. They
would not have listened to such preaching any more complacently than
John Knox.

Let us bring the pulpit to its true test, though the human work be
burned, and though the preacher be saved as by fire. Lay it open to the
light, as it appears by the side of the simplicity, the directness, the timeli-
ness, the sacredness, and the intensity of truth as used by the Holy Spirit
in the salvation of souls. There lies the proof of a living pulpit. Confronted with such an ideal, the affectations I have described shrivel into
nothingness. Vanity of vanities, saith the preacher; all is vanity! They are
false to the very titles in which their praise is so often vaunted. They are

not "sound"; they are not "scholarly"; they are not "eloquent"; they are not "churchly"; they are not "beautiful"; they are not "finished"; they are not "in good taste"; for—they are not good sense. And they are not good sense because they are not subdued by awe of truth, as God's instrument, put into the preacher's hand for ends which it is impiety to neglect. No matter how much truth may be wrapped up in these false arts, souls never feel it; the preacher does not feel it. Neither can be quickened by it, any more than corpses in arctic seas can feel the latent caloric of the ice-fields which have congealed their life-blood.

Repose in Truth

When one of those useful pastors, who are "not eloquent," encounters ungenial criticism, it is his right to rest calmly upon his calling of God to the preaching of truth. No secret distrust should impair the joy of such a preacher in his work. There is a certain trust in God's word that truth shall do its work in the hearts of men, which every preacher needs to make him a man of power. It is an equable and joyous trust. It is a spirit of repose in the destiny of the instrument which God has chosen. Once possessed of it, and possessed by it, a preacher feels that he can afford to preach truth truthfully. He need not exaggerate truth. He need not distort it. He need not deck it with meretricious ornament. He need not surround it with eccentric illustration. He need not swathe it in transcendental speech. He need not belabor it with theatrical declamation. He need not mince it, nor trim it, nor inflate it, nor paint it. He has only to preach it, thoughtfully, vividly, variously, and with the singleness of an intense soul living in communion with God, and then let it do its own work. It will do its work. He may have faith in it. In the midst of exhausting toils, when wearied with that stern suppression of fitful hopes and apprehensions which must enter largely into every intense life, he may find this spirit of repose in truth falling upon him like the mantle of a prophet. He may know then that his words are the wisdom of God and the power of God. He will often speak with the consciousness of that which is a pledge of his success. He will speak with a daring neglect of false expedients and conventionalities, which will astonish men who do not know where is the hiding of his power.

We are told that Napoleon in battle used to be restless, anxious, irritable, and taciturn, till a certain critical point was reached in the execution of his orders; but that after that crisis was past, —a crisis invisible to all eyes but his, — and long before any prospect of victory appeared to his subordinates, he suddenly became calm, bland in his manners, apparently careless in his maneuvers, even jovial in his conversation; and at the battle of Eylau, at the risk of defeat, as others judged, he lay down to sleep on a hillock, which the enemy's grape-shot grazed without wakening him. In explanation of his hardihood, he said that there was a turning-point in all his plans of battle beyond which, if it were safely reached, he deemed victory secure. He knew then that he could not lose the day. His work was done.

The repose of genius in the assurance of results which are invisible to inferior minds, can bear no comparison with that rest in the power of truth which a preacher may feel, and which, if he does feel it reasonably, will go far towards realizing his expectations of success. The secret of his power will be simply that he is proclaiming God's truth, at God's bidding, and in God's methods. He gives to men that which God has given to him. The cloud of the Divine Presence envelops him. Within that august protection he performs his life's work. He cannot but achieve results which God will own. He may labor trustfully, for he must succeed. No man ever failed who preached thus. The world may never know his power; but he shall know it; and God shall one day proclaim it, at that tribunal at which shall be fulfilled those words so pregnant with the decisions of eternity upon the history of the pulpit: "There are last which shall be first, and there are first which shall be last."

Chapter 4

Responsibility As Related to Sovereignty

The most serious difficulties of religion cluster around certain points of union of doctrines which are opposites, but not contraries, in the system of truth. They stand over against each other for a double purpose: by their differences each defines the outline and reflects the excellence of the other, and by their harmony both magnify the honor of the Author of truth, as neither could do alone.

Such correlative truths are numerous around the point of junction of Divine with human agencies. The difficulties of our faith therefore grow dense around the doctrines of Providence, of Prayer, of Predestination, and perhaps most of all around that of Regeneration. The power of such difficulties depends very much upon the spirit with which they are approached. Three principles, especially, should govern inquiry on such a theme.

First, that inquiry should be conducted with reverence for the prerogatives of God. It is as much the dictate of sober judgment as of a pure conscience to preserve that jealousy in behalf of the divine honor which the apostle expressed when he said: "Let God be true, though every man a liar." Again, in such an inquiry we should expect to come upon insoluble mystery; not absurdity, but mystery; not contradictions, but mystery. Who knows the spirit of a man? A child propounds questions concerning it which no man can answer. To whom then will ye liken God? Canst thou by searching find the Almighty out unto perfection? When therefore from two such fountains the streams emanate which are commingled in human destiny, shall we expect to find nothing that appeals to faith? In the confluence of two such powers, is it marvellous that to our vision the waters are troubled?

Furthermore, in such an inquiry we should be content with the removal of practical difficulties. It is a principle which the wisest of men have acknowledged in respect to things other than religion, that those perplexities which start out of metaphysical science should never be allowed to confuse us in the practical affairs of life. Men who have believed in the non-existence of matter have yet eaten and drunk and slept and walked like their neighbors. Men who have been unable to see the evidence of their existence have yet been very sensitive if other men were as ignorant. Yet, in religious inquiry the human mind exhibits a proneness to disregard this principle of common sense, by wandering away from plain matters of fact, and, as Isaac Taylor has expressed it, "to beat up and down through regions of night, from which their only escape must be, by a buoyant effort of good sense, to spring up from the abyss to the trodden and familiar surface of things."

With these principles in mind, let us consider the responsibility of man as related to the agency of God in conversion.

I. Difficulties of the Subject Practical

Let us, in the first place, discern clearly the reality of the difficulty which an inquiring sinner often feels respecting his own responsibility for a result which is still dependent on Almighty power. The difficulty is practical. It is felt by minds which know little, and care less, about philosophical abstractions. Every pastor is familiar with it in the popular experience. No inquiry is pressed with deeper solicitude by a certain class of minds than this: How can these things be? "You tell me," is often the language of their hearts, "you tell me that I must be born again. I must have a new heart and a new spirit. To produce this change is the work of God. You portray this change to me in language which is itself an appalling expression of my dependence upon invisible and almighty will for its achievement. My puny faculties are frightened at the conception of a change from darkness to light, from death to life, and from the power of Satan to that of God. Why, then, do you summon me to any duty in this emergency? What have I to do but to await the revelation of that eternal decree on which my destiny hangs in suspense, like that of a mote upon the law of gravitation? How can I repent? How can I believe? Am I not shut up to this one resource: to stand in dumb agony before the Will, as one of your own most venerable theologians has termed it, the *arbitrary* Will, of God? He hath mercy on whom he will have mercy." An oppressive significance is sometimes crowded into the words: What must I do to be saved? They are often the outburst of a hopeless intellect, as well as of a burdened conscience.

That this is not an extravagant statement of the practical character of the difficulties which many feel on this subject, will be obvious to anyone who is familiar with the unrecorded experience of inquirers, when they are made to stand face to face with the doctrine of the sovereignty of God in their salvation.

In confirmation and in illustration of this statement, I may be permitted to refer to the experience of one who subsequently became a preacher. In an unpublished communication to a friend, some years after his conversion, he wrote respecting this theme as follows: "Few subjects open to me a deeper abyss than this. The attempt to speak of it recalls to me a period of my life when I can truly say: 'The pains of hell got hold upon me.' I think I know the difficulties of a sinner burdened by his dependence upon a power out of himself for salvation. I have been all over that land of darkness and of the, shadow of death. I have seen those difficulties piled up like Alps on Alps. I recall seven months of my life in which my mind beat about that thought of dependence upon the grace of God without a ray of light or of hope. I searched the Scriptures. I read books of devotion. I conversed with theologians. I ransacked their libraries for some explanation of the mystery which appeared to me then to be a contradiction to my natural ideas of justice. The gloom it created reached at last every part of God's word: I could read no hope, there. It covered all Nature: I could see no justice there. Sleep became more desirable to me than waking. The morning only woke me to a consciousness of misery; and the feeling excited in me by the sight of the busy world around me was a kind of bitter compassion that so many of them must soon end their little dream of life, and then awake to a wretchedness as complete as mine."

II. THE SENSE OF RESPONSIBILITY AN INTUITION

Conceding, then, the practical character of the perplexities which often surround the conjunction of these two ideas of responsibility and of dependence in the way of salvation, let us observe that Responsibility, in any development of it, must rest primarily upon a species of independent evidence which a sound mind cannot resist. A man's own consciousness is the root of the matter. God has so constituted accountable being, that what it is is wrought into the consciousness that it is. Nothing can go below this; nothing can outrun this. Reasoning here can add nothing to knowledge. Analysis of free-agency can furnish no additional evidence of the fact. Dissection of the body discovers no evidence of vitality. No man can thus demonstrate his own responsibility; yet no man can rid himself of the conviction that he is responsible. This is the primal conviction of our moral being. It is to moral existence what the optic nerve is to the eye. It is one of those "high instincts".

> "Which, be they what they may,
> Are yet the fountain light of all our day;
> Are yet a master light of all our seeing:
>
> Truths that wake
> To perish never,
> Which neither listlessness nor mad endeavor
> Can utterly abolish or destroy."

It stays by us when we would fling it from us. It follows hard after us when we would flee from the sight of it. Something holds us to it more vigorous than logic. We cannot escape it; it is part of us. It is wrought into the structure of every language. Philosophers have reasoned it down; they have voted it out of the world by sage majorities; but the world will not let it go, nor will it let the world go, so long as the word "ought" is intelligible to a sane mind.

On this basis of *knowledge,* then, rests the responsibility of any man, regarded as the general condition of his being. But on the very same basis rests the responsibility of an awakened sinner for instant, absolute, and entire obedience to God's commands; and this at the very hour of his perplexities on the subject of a change of heart. No mind can possess more convincing evidence of its responsibility than that mind which is aroused to ask: "What must I do to be saved?" Such a one knows his responsibility for everything that God requires of him, as with open eye he knows light. Every pang of conviction proves this; every fear proves this. He is *conscious* of guilt in having been a sinner; he is *conscious* of guilt in being a sinner; he is *conscious* of guilt in continuing to be a sinner. His want of penitence is a sin to him. His want of love to God is a sin to him. The guilt is his own; he *feels* it rankling in his own soul. God could not affirm to him his responsibility more distinctly than by the voice of that angered conscience. If that truth were written in the heavens it could be no more authoritative. A revelation of it by one risen from the dead could make it no more sacred. He never has a more imperative disclosure of it to his soul than when his convictions of sin are most home-felt, and his fear of eternity most intolerable. Black as may be the abyss in which the philosophy of regeneration seems to leave him, he cannot doubt the fact of his responsibility for being there, and for ceasing to be there at God's bidding. If he seems to himself to doubt this, he is like an insane man who questions his own existence, and recounts to you the narrative of his own death and burial. The remark of Dr. Johnson upon the philosophical question of freedom is as truthful respecting the fact of a sinner's responsibility for all that God requires of him in salvation "A man knows it, sir, and that is the whole of it."

III. RESPONSIBILITY NOT DESTROYED BY DEPRAVITY

It is instructive to observe the confidence which the human mind reposes in its knowledge of its own responsibility as this confidence is exhibited in the fact, that the common sense of men never attributes to sin, however passionate or obdurate, the power to destroy responsibility. The infatuation of guilt never even impairs, in a healthy mind, the sense of the enormity of guilt. However rooted crime becomes, as if in the very nature of the criminal, until we say of him in loose dialect: It is his nature to lie, to steal, to murder; he does not know how to do otherwise; evil has possession of him; he hath a devil: yet we never in such modes of speech hold a sinner guiltless; we never loosen the gripe of responsibility upon his being. We still say, with the wise man: "His own iniquities shall take the wicked himself; and he shall be holden with the cords of his sins." Penal jurisprudence in civilized law is built upon this principal. It laughs at the fiction of moral insanity as a product of guilt.

Let this principle be illustrated in an occurrence which is yet fresh in our national history. We were told, a few years ago, of a man who sat in the councils of the country, the representative, as he said, of a gallant people; we were told that, under the impulse of revenge, he violated the laws of justice, of honor, of courage, and of civilized humanity, of all that a gallant people should respect. We heard — and did not our ears tingle at the story?—we heard that he crept stealthily, and armed to the teeth, into the highest legislative sanctuary of the land, and there, awaiting his time like an assassin, he felled to the floor a solitary, unarmed, and pinioned man; a man his superior in age, in official rank, in refinement of taste, in classic learning, in patriotism, in integrity of conscience, in all that can dignify a gentleman and a statesman.

Yet the gallant assassin told us: "I meant no wrong; I was conscious of no crime; I purposed only to inflict the chastisement which I would give to a servant or a dog." But what was our answer? We said by the mouth of one of our representatives, as you may remember: "That was a brutal and cowardly and murderous deed." Yet the noble assassin condescended to say to us: "No, oh no! you do me wrong; I did not know the force of the blows I struck; it was but a reed that I held in my hand; and that first blow aroused the demon in my heart; after that, I knew not what I did; and it was well for him, yes, it was well for him, that he did not resist my fury." Put again, what was our answer? We compressed it with indignant lips; we said of the august assassin: "He smote his victim as Cain did his brother."

Did we not believe those words? Did we not hold the man to be a man, and therefore responsible for his blindfold conscience, and his infuriated passion, and for all the consequences? Did we not hold him guilty for not knowing what he did? Did we not believe it to have been his own spirit that was the demon in his heart? Was it not a free demon? Was it not a voluntary demon? Was it not a responsible demon? Who believes that he was unable to resist the impulses of that demoniacal possession? When the eyes of twenty millions flashed fire, and their lips execrated the deed, was it in rebuke of a poor lunatic who had strayed from the tombs? When the echo of those blows came back to us from the other side of the Atlantic, in the outcry of the civilized world, from Gibraltar to Siberia, against the barbarism of American institutions, was it a mistaken cruelty towards one whose dwelling was with the beasts of the field, and who did eat grass like oxen? Oh no, no! The common conscience of the world answers, No. The common sense of the world responds, No. The reverberation of cannon and the tramp of a million armed men have protested, No. Impartial history will confirm the verdict, No. Thoughtful men, but a few months after, stood around an open grave. They shut their mouths in awe-struck silence. That which had not been told them, they saw; that which they had not heard, did they consider. They thought within themselves: Here lies a poor, deluded, blinded, infatuated sinner, but still a deluded sinner, a blinded sinner, an infatuated sinner. They thought of the verdict sometimes rendered at an inquest to which death has not given up its secret: "Died by visitation of God." Christian minds, the world over, when they heard of that untimely end, remembered God's own decree: "Bloody and deceitful men shall not live out half their days." And all the people said, "Amen." So impossible is it to stultify the moral convictions of the world, by the figment of a moral responsibility destroyed by the obduracy or the passionateness of guilt.

IV. BIBLICAL THEORY OF RESPONSIBILITY

The authority of revelation is added to that of conscience in testimony to the truth before us. The Scriptures hold man responsible for a compliance with the conditions of salvation. They hold him to account for the entire character which renders salvation a fact. This has never been intelligently questioned. It is one of the points of indubitable and unbroken alliance between revelation and conscience. The word of God is here but the echo of his work. The Scriptures hold a sinner, an unregenerate sinner, responsible for repentance of sin and for faith in Christ, and for everything else which is a constituent of a regenerate character. No hint is given that this responsibility is at all dependent on the gift of regenerating grace. Duties and graces are urged upon the natural consciences of men, with no qualification whatever. To an unsophisticated reader, men seem to be exhorted to repent and believe, to love, to trust, to obey, to adore, to praise, to be perfect as God is perfect, with the same freedom with which they are commanded to refrain from lying, from stealing, from murder. The inspired writers treat the whole subject with a boldness which is often startling, and yet refreshing, by the side of some of the wary and diplomatic methods of catechetical theology. They do not seem to have been embarrassed by their own equally bold conceptions of the sovereignty of God.

One whose mind has wandered over the immensity of these themes, with no practical object by which to test its convictions, and on which to concentrate them, may be astonished at the daring with which the inspired writers use the truths at which philosophy has stood aghast. It is the usual method of inspiration to assume the responsibility of a sinner, and to urge upon him the duties of repentance, of faith, of submission, of perfect obedience, unqualified by any mention whatever of his dependence upon God. Duty is urged as if a sinner had no concern with anything else than duty. Yet turn a leaf, and we see absolute dependence and eternal decree unrolled like the scroll of fate, with no proviso to save the freedom of a man; as if decree and dependence were the only pillars of God's government. If we are timid lest our theological formulae should be unravelled in the process, we tremble when we read: "Wash you, make you clean"; "Without me ye can do nothing": "Make to yourselves a new heart"; "Our sufficiency is of God": "Repent and be converted"; "He hath mercy on whom he will have mercy": "Submit yourselves unto God"; "And whom he will he hardeneth": "Work out your own salvation"; "It is God that worketh in you": "Awake, thou that sleepest"; "The Lord hath poured upon you the spirit of a deep sleep": "Believe on the Lord Jesus Christ"; "God shall send them delusion, that they should believe a lie"; "Turn ye, turn ye, for why will ye die!" "That they all might be damned which believe not the truth."

Pages of these paradoxical responses might be compiled from the Scriptures. Are we prompt to exclaim: This is more than paradox; it is contradiction? It is such contradiction as Paul indulges when he says: "We are deceivers, yet true; unknown, yet well known; dying, yet we live; sorrowful, yet always rejoicing; poor, yet making many rich; having nothing, yet possessing all things." Such verbal contradictions are the profoundest harmonies. They are the index of a masculine grasp of truth. It is not the way of great souls, moved by great truths, to be content with conceptions which can be sifted clean of paradox, and their residuum measured with algebraic exactness. Great truths have caverns of thought which lie below scientific language; and great minds are ever exploring those recesses. Thus it is with inspiration, which is only the greatness of divine thought. Inspired conception holds these opposites of truth with no sense of contradiction. A serenity of faith pervades the inspired thought upon them, like the tranquillity which no tempest breaks at the bottom of the Atlantic. When such thought comes to be expressed in speech, it refuses qualifications and provisoes. It takes on bold and craggy forms. It loves the mind that dares to speak it outright, and then leave it in the majesty of its singleness. Such is the celestial calmness with which inspired minds have dealt with the responsibility of man. They betray no sense of shame at their heedlessness of the divine honor in urging the claims of duty with an importunity which seems to forget all else than duty. A doubt of the completeness of man's responsibility for the discharge of his duty, and of the whole of it, is never tolerated by them. Those difficulties of inquiry which, if they mean anything, signify an implication of injustice in holding man accountable under the law of sovereignty, are met with rebuke rather than with reasoning: "Who art thou, O man, that repliest against God?"

V. ABILITY THE MEASURE OF OBLIGATION

From the authoritative tone with which both the consciousness of men and the word of God thus teach the responsibility of unregenerate mind, we are led to infer the ability of an unregenerate sinner to obey all the divine commands which are laid upon him.

What precisely do we mean by this? That an unregenerate mind, remaining unregenerate, can obey God? No; we do not so trifle with contradiction in terms. The carnal mind is not subject to the law of God, neither indeed can be. A man with closed eyes does not see a precipice at mid-day, neither indeed can he see it; one step therefore may plunge him to the bottom. But he can open his eyes; what then? Is there no difference between a man with voluntarily closed eyes and a blind man? Is there none between a man who will not see and a man born blind? So, we do not deny the truism that a sinner remaining impenitent cannot repent; he cannot be and not be at the same moment. But he can choose not to remain impenitent, what then? Is there no difference between a sinner who cannot because he will not repent, and a sinner who cannot because he is "disabled" to will otherwise? Is there none between one who cannot because he will not and one who is born disabled? We use language, then, in the strict and proper sense of it, as the common mind interprets it, when we affirm the inevitable inference from human consciousness and the word of God, that an unregenerate sinner can obey all the commands of God.

"I Can, Because I Ought"

A child's book exists in our Sabbath-school literature, with the simple yet profoundly philosophic title: "I can, because I ought." The fresh mind of childhood never denied the truth expressed in those words. The conscience of a child must be awed down by authority into unnatural contortions, before it will create the feeling or the belief of guilt in that child's heart for that which he did not originate and cannot control.

"I can, because I ought:" Ability—the necessary inference from obligation; obligation—the measure of ability. The central truth which gives value to the tomes of theological lore on this subject is compressed into those words. It is impossible that reasoning should go below it or around it with the purpose of evasion. It is ultimate; thought can go no farther. We reason around and around the immensity of the theme, and an invisible thread conducts us through the labyrinth back to the point at which we started, and at which every child can see as far as the keenest of us.

"I can, because I ought:" we struggle to go by this truth; we traverse the universe in our philosophic search for something beyond it; but at the circumference of our journey we have not outrun it, any more than we can outrun the evening star in search for the horizon. We plunge into the depths of our own being in quest of something which consciousness may have treasured up beneath it, but at the bottom of all things we find it awaiting us, "a gem of purest ray serene."

"I can, because I ought:" it is one of those truths which we carry with us because it is a part of us. We cannot look into any mirror of truth without seeing the reflection of it. It is like an omnipresent Deity. It is indeed the voice of God within us. We may say of it "Thou hast beset me behind and before; thou hast laid thy hand upon me. Whither shall I go from thy spirit? whither shall I flee from thy presence? If I ascend up into heaven, thou art there; if I make my bed in hell, behold thou art there; if I take the wings of the morning and dwell in the uttermost parts of the sea, even there shall thy hand lead me: yea, the darkness and the light are both alike to thee. Thou hast possessed my reins: I am fearfully and wonderfully made."

"I can, because I ought." This, then, is the conviction with which an inquiring sinner must meet the question of his own salvation. I can obey, because God requires me to obey. I can repent, because I feel guilty for not repenting. God would not demand of me to do what I cannot do.

God would never have so constituted my being that I must feel guilty for not doing what I cannot do.

Ability, the Teaching of Common Sense

This is the irresistible reasoning of any unsophisticated mind. The common sense of the world reasons so without hesitation and without exception. Teach your child that he has lied to you because he could not help it, and will he justify your rod? Teach a thief that he stole because the necessity of his avaricious nature was upon him, and will he look up self-condemned to your barred windows and bolted doors and armed sentinels? Teach a murderer that he shed the blood of his victim because he was the victim of an insane malignity over which he had no power, and will he confess the awful excellence of justice on your scaffold? If he does, it will be simply because he knows better than your teachings.

So, proclaim to an inquiring sinner that he is a sinner because he cannot be anything else; that he hates God because it is his nature to hate God; that he is a depraved being and a child of wrath because he was born such; that he does not repent because he is impotent to repent; that he does not obey God because the power is not in him to obey God; that therefore if he is not saved it is because God has not elected him to salvation; and will he feel the damning guilt of his condition, the equity of his doom, the awful righteousness of the coming judgment? If he does so, it will be because conscience and the Holy Ghost are mightier than your theology. Never, never does reason draw such conclusion from such premises. The common sense of the world never reasons so.

The common sense, moreover, refuses to be mystified in its reasonings by any distinction between power in character and power in act; between power to be and power to do. To the popular mind, if a man cannot he cannot; and that is the end of it. Obligation, guilt, just condemnation, remorse, punishment honorable to law — not one of these can co-exist with impotence in the being of whom they are affirmed. No matter whether the sinfulness in question be innate depravity or that of an act of murder; the reasoning of the common sense is the same. Inability to be all that God requires is a bar to the justice of requirement, as absolute as inability to withhold the stroke of a dagger is to the justice of the gibbet. An "insane murderer" is no more an impossible contradiction in any civilized court of law than a "disabled sinner" is at the bar of God. We count it to the honor of our humane civilization that our asylums, more sacred than "cities of refuge" from the avenger of blood, are thrown open to the insane homicide, and he is reverently cared for as a brother on whom the hand of God rests. If then it be conceivable that, any where in the universe, there are moral beings who are "disabled unto all good," shall not He whose ways are equal and whose name is Love find, somewhere among the still planets, a retreat where those afflicted spirits may hide themselves till their tangled and broken faculties shall be allured back again into symmetry and wholeness? Shall such beings be left to call on the rocks and mountains to hide them from the face of Him that sitteth on the throne? Whose reason would not reel if this were true?

Thus, be it repeated, thus reasons the common sense of men. There is no sense in reasoning otherwise. If the opposite conviction is established, it must be by authority, not by reasoning. But it is unsafe to question, on any authority, such a primal conviction of the soul. It is hazardous to the integrity of mind in all its operations. It hoodwinks perception of right and wrong. It blunts sensibility to good and evil. It deadens, therefore, the soul's response to the nature of God as a God of equity and of judgment.

Moreover, such a denial of the mind's necessary belief is unphilosophical. So to use any conceivable authority as to array it by sheer power against a first principle of belief, is to defeat that very authority in the very act of its assertion; for the foundation of all authority over intelligent belief is inundated and swept away in the process. Faith has then no more bottom to stand on than reason. Both go to wreck together. If I cannot trust one necessary belief, I cannot another. I have nothing left, on which to build faith in a revelation. My soul then sinks in unbelief to depths immeasurable, in which all that it knows is that it knows nothing, believes nothing, hopes nothing. To borrow a similitude, such denial of ability to obey a command of God is, to the whole structure of a moral being, like the magnetic mountain to the navigator in the Arabian story. As he sailed alongside of it, it drew out the clamping-irons of his vessel, and the timbers fell asunder, and the ship was wrecked, though in still waters on a summer's day.

Once more, "I can, because I ought." We cast reflection upon God's honor if we deny this in respect of obedience to his commands in the way of salvation. We implicate the word of God in a collision with his works; and we involve his work, in the structure of a soul, in a more awful conflict with itself. We should be jealous for the divine prerogative in this thing. Shall the thing formed have reason to say unto Him that formed it: "Why hast thou made me thus?"

VI. RESPONSIBILITY AND SOVEREIGNTY HARMONIOUS

We are prepared, then, to observe that in this view of responsibility there is no conflict with the truth of a sinner's dependence upon the Holy Spirit. Reason affirms no conflict here any more than revelation. If a sinner is not dependent on regenerating grace for ability to do his duty, he is not dependent on regenerating grace for anything that is essential to responsibility for the performance of his duty. If dependence is not for the power but for the will to obey, reason has no more difficulty than faith in determining responsibility. Not only is no contradiction proved, but none is suggested between, responsibility and dependence. We cannot properly speak of reconciling these truths; we can discern no variance between them to be removed. Our conceptions of them fall into the same ease and harmony of thought in which they seem to have lain in inspired minds.

The dependence of a being who is responsible because able to do all that God requires of him, is no more the dependence of necessity, but the dependence of sheer guilt. It is not the dependence of a diseased man upon the herb that shall restore him. It is not the dependence of a disabled man upon the surgeon who shall set the broken limb. It is not the dependence of the man with a withered hand upon the miracle that shall make it whole like the other. It is the dependence of a perverse man, who of himself will not be other than a perverse man, upon the power that shall incline him to obedience. It is the dependence of a liar, who of himself will not be other than a liar, upon the influences that induce him to be truthful. It is the dependence of a murderer, who of himself will not be other than a murderer, upon the friend who shall persuade him to put up his dagger into its sheath. This, which in kind, and when applied to elemental changes of character, is the most profound and terrific dependence under which a moral being can exist, stands side by side with responsible being, with no collision, with not a breath of discord between them. The two thoughts are like angels locked hand in hand, in ministering to God's will and vindicating his ways to men.

Is it still said that mystery hangs over the whole conception of a being who can but will not be other than a sinner until God constrains him? True; it is the great marvel of the universe that any being will not obey God. Is it said that mystery covers the junction of Divine influence with human power in the change of a sinner's heart? True; and the savage fled in terror from the artist's studio when he first saw his own portrait, because he could not understand the mystery of the artist's pencil, which could so represent him on the canvas without abstracting a part of him. Is it said that mystery buries in darkness the turning-point of character at which a sinner becomes a changed being; a sinner who now, without God, will not be other than a sinner, yet then, through God, is a believer; who now will not but be a child of wrath, yet then is an heir of glory; that we cannot penetrate to the heart of this? True; great is the mystery of godliness. And not unlike this mystery is the fact that a man cannot see the power of his own vision; cannot look at the nerve which lies back of his own eyeball; cannot take in his hand the filament which connects that nerve with the spiritual seer who is behind it. But mystery is not contradiction. It is not even a seeming contradiction. An apparent absurdity is an absurdity to us until we believe, and have reason to believe, it to be only apparent. Mystery is not this; it is only a hint of magnitude. We must fall back, therefore, upon the conviction of responsibility for guilt, and of the dependence of guilt, as upon two of the elemental truths on which rests the government of God over our world. We may think and speak of them at our ease, without the most secret suspicion of their inconsistency, or fear of a collision. We may preach them as inspired men have preached them, with intensity of conception, with boldness of speech, with singleness of aim. These are the only methods in which they can be preached by men who are in earnest.

VII. "What must I Do to Be Saved?"

Some of the results of this discussion bear specifically upon the methods of the pulpit and of Christian teachers in addressing inquirers after the way of salvation.

The answer to the inquiry, "What must I do to be saved?" would appear to be very simple in view of the history of the inquiry in the Scriptures. There, it is the inquiry of unsophisticated minds, and the outburst of burdened hearts. No philosophic theories of conversion, venerated as the growth of ages, lay back of it. It came forth, fresh from souls which were in downright earnest to do something for their salvation, if they might but know what to do. They were satisfied, therefore, and the inspired teacher assumed that they ought to be satisfied, with an answer which was as direct, as earnest, and as free from mysticism as their question was.

It needs hardly to be said, that modern inquirers after the way of salvation, in Christian lands at least, come to the subject in a very different way. They approach it through the avenue of a different mental history. The novelty of Christian thought is commonly worn away before they reach that crisis in which the question of religious destiny is to be decided. They bring to it a multitude of preconceptions. Inherited beliefs, the mental deposits of education, and the relics of former religious awakenings are mingled with the mental habits of impenitence. The true and the false are intertwined intricately. Inquiry itself, under such conditions, is not free from sophistry. The stereotyped language in which it expresses itself may be more largely an imitation than an experience. It may not mean all that it seems to mean.

The work of a religious teacher, therefore, in the instruction of religious inquirers, is often one of delicate complications. Simple as it is in its results, it has no such simplicity in its methods as if we were at liberty to inundate the whole past of the inquirer's mind and sweep it away by teaching the rudiments of a new religion. We must save to him much that is true and salutary in his experience. Yet we must often extricate him from mental confusion, by clearing his way back to certain first principles of truth, which his experience has obscured. Several of these principles are very clearly established by the present discussion.

Repentance and Faith Practicable, like Other Duties

One such principle is, that we should urge upon men the performance of the conditions of salvation, with the same unrestricted freedom of speech with which we would press the discharge of any other duty.

Men should be invited, persuaded, entreated, commanded to repent and believe, with the same unqualified boldness with which we should teach them to speak the truth, to pay an honest debt, to befriend the widow and the fatherless. Responsibility is as perfect in the one class of duties as in the other. Duty is as absolute. The responsibility in both cases rests upon the same immutable basis—the intrinsic justice of a Divine command, and the indestructible ability of man to obey. The sinner is responsible for repentance and faith to the full extent of Divine requirement, simply because God requires them and because the sinner is able to render them.

We should seek to penetrate with this conviction the soul of every man who would know what he must do to be saved. We owe it to the simplicity of the truth to clear it of contradictions in the troubled thoughts of an inquirer. We should strip it of factitious mystery. We should let the absolute sacredness of Duty, backed by the sanctions of Eternity, come home to the conscience in words simple and few, without qualification or proviso.

The fiction of inability to obey a command of God, with which an inquiring mind is often blinded, should be commonly treated as a Satanic suggestion. That conviction of inability does not exist often in such a mind in the forms of metaphysic and theologic statement, in which technical definition makes the fiction a truth. A mind oppressed by fear of hell is in no mood, commonly, to appreciate our philosophical distinction between "natural" and "moral" inability. The plea of inability by which a convicted sinner parries duty, exists in the plain, homely sense of words which mean to the distracted soul just what they seem to mean in literal speech. "Cannot," is "cannot;" nothing more, nothing less. It conveys but one idea. That idea has to him no metaphysical double sense. It is intensely literal, and as intensely false. It arrays Conscience and Fact, God and Truth, in defiant hostility to each other. The sinner says to his soul: "God commands me to do this thing—I cannot; God commands me to repent—I cannot; God commands me to believe—I cannot. He commands, knowing that I cannot obey. It is as if he commanded me to restore the lost Pleiad." This conviction, we repeat, in this unscientific form in which it holds inquiring souls in bondage, should be treated as a stupendous delusion. The inquirer should be thrown back upon the imperative teachings of the Scriptures and of the common sense. He should be made to feel that in cherishing such a sense of impotence he is clinging to the refuge of a falsehood. He is stultifying his own reason, defying his own conscience, and charging God with crime. We have no right, my brethren, we have no right as teachers of truth, to suffer a sinner to go from our instructions to the bar of God, in the dilemma of either falsifying his reason or repudiating his conscience, and therefore with all the forces of truth thrown into panic in his soul, through the contradiction of his necessary beliefs to our delivery of God's commands.

It is unphilosophical and unsafe, as well as unscriptural, to teach the duty of repentance less imperatively than inspired men have taught it. We have no authority to lengthen or to soften the peremptory words of the Holy Ghost. We should not so far yield to the fiction of inability as to say to the inquiring sinner: "Repent if you can; try to repent; repent of such sins as you can repent of; use the means of repentance; pray that you may be enabled to repent"; and to *say no more*. It is neither reasonable nor scriptural to entice a sinner up thus to a side-look upon his duty, and *leave him there*. He should be led around to the front, and urged to face the truth in its imperative singleness—"Repent"; and this with the full force of the implication, and if need be the statement, that he can repent. With Divine grace or without it, regenerate or unregenerate, elect or non-elect, his responsibility is as perfect as God can make it. Radically, it does not depend on Divine grace. Temptation does not fundamentally affect it. "God doth not suffer you to be tempted above that ye are able." The unregenerate sinner should be taught that *he has the power to do anything which God has the will to command*. We never get the unbroken force of Conscience over to the side of truth otherwise.

Dependence of Guilt and the Dependence of Necessity

But is not the teaching of an unqualified responsibility perilous? Will not a sinner be tempted to revel in his freedom? Will he not say within himself: "My soul is my own; salvation is in my own power; I have but to will it, and Heaven is at my bidding; Soul, thou hast much goods laid up for many years in this power to repent at thy pleasure; take thine ease"? Perhaps so; what distortion will not sin prompt in evasion or in caricature of truth? Yet God does not therefore abolish the perils of probation. It were sufficient to say that He who spake as never man spake thus preached repentance in bold and unguarded words. But here, as elsewhere, truth carries its own safeguards. For —

A second consequence of the principles we have considered is, that we should proclaim the dependence of a sinner upon the Holy Ghost for the will to repent, as being a more profound reality than if it were dependence for the power to repent.

Two methods are here suggested regarding the doctrine of Divine

Sovereignty. They may have the same end in view, may be adopted with equal conscientiousness, and may be prompted by the same devout desire to honor God. Yet they are very unequal in the depth to which they penetrate truth, and the force with which they use it. They are very dissimilar also in the skill with which they avoid perversions of the truth in the result. The one method is, to exalt the sovereignty of God in salvation as a work of mere Power. The other is, to exalt the sovereignty of God in salvation as a work of Moral Government. In the one case, God is made to appear sovereign of a sinner's destiny, as he is of the elements in a tempest. He can say to the passions of guilt, Be still; and they shall obey him. His sway of the soul is like his sway of the sea. Both are exhibitions of power—grand; magnificent, overwhelming it may be, but still power, and that only. The final impression of the beholder is that of the glory of Omnipotence.

In the other case, God is represented as sovereign in the work of salvation under the conditions of a moral system. He ordained those conditions from eternity. They are sacred to him. His own integrity is pledged to them. He cannot violate them with impunity to his own consciousness of rectitude. They were planned in the counsels of eternity for the display of his moral glory as supreme over his natural perfections. His sway of a soul, therefore, is unique. It is like nothing else in the heavens above, or in the earth beneath, or in the waters under the earth. It is not an exercise of power only. The final impression upon a beholder is not that of omnipotence supremely, but of omnipotence in the service of justice, holiness, truth, love. It is that of infinite power regulated by infinite integrity. The perspective of the system is so adjusted that the spectator shall look through the natural to the moral disclosures of the Divine glory. He sees, not unlimited Force driving before it an insensate thing, but infinite Holiness swaying a free mind, through all the sinuosities of its choice, by the delicate, intricate, and balanced working of moral laws.

Now, the difference between these two methods of representing the sovereignty of God in salvation is vital. It corresponds to *the difference between Might and Right*. It is just the difference between appeal to the sense of weakness and appeal to the sense of sin. It is vitally significant to religious teaching in several respects. In the first place, we can much more easily impress upon men a sense of the sovereignty of might than that of the sovereignty of right. A fallen mind takes in the idea of a God of power more spontaneously than that of a God of rectitude. Again, an awakened soul, agitated by fear, is specially receptive of the truth of Divine Power; yet that soul goaded by remorse, and quick to spring to anything that shall help it to fling elsewhere the load of its guilt, is specially impervious to the truth of Divine integrity. A God sovereign by might is less uncongenial with the bitterness of its spirit than a God sovereign by right. Still further, the drift of a tempted soul is to accept the conviction of God's power at the *expense* of his justice. The leanings of guilt are all one way. Subjection to an infinite tyranny is less revolting to it than submission to infinite equity.

Is there, then, no peril indicated here to our conceptions of Divine Sovereignty? Is there no danger that the scriptural proportions of truth may become distorted in the portraiture we draw of the Divine government? What if, in our solicitude to exalt the power of God, we so depict it that we unwittingly elevate it above his holiness? Is there no danger then? What if we so imperiously proclaim his omnipotence over a guilty soul that the practical impression upon that soul obscures all sense of his equity, his sincerity, his honor, his love? Is there no risk then? What if we so speak as God's vicegerents, that, though unconscious of any such design, we throw out discordant fragments of the truth this way and that, and they happen to fall in with the cavils of a tempted spirit, and seem to consolidate its sense of sheer dominion at the expense of all the holy and amiable attributes of God in his moral government? Is there no hazard there? What if, to make sure that the Divine authority shall not be understated, we seem, though we should be shocked by the imputation of any such purpose, yet we seem to the common sense of our hearers to build God's government upon principles which would doom any human government on earth to execration? Is there no peril in that?

Yet, from these two methods of regarding Divine sovereignty arise corresponding methods of representing the dependence of a sinner upon the Holy Spirit for salvation. By the one method, it is the dependence of necessity; by the other, the dependence of guilt. The dependence is absolute in either case. No interest of truth is served by ignoring or retrenching that. So long as a sinner will not repent without Divine grace, his dependence upon that grace is as perfect in degree, though not the same in kind, as if he could not repent. But because it is not the same in kind, the moral significance of it is unspeakably the more intense. As necessity knows no law, so the dependence of necessity knows no guilt. It has no moral significance. Not so the dependence which our subject teaches. The very groundwork of this is guilt, and guilt only. Thus we should proclaim it. We should so sketch a sinner's dependence upon the Holy Ghost as to keep the moral rectitude of God in the foreground of his power. The helplessness of which we seek to make the sinner conscious should be, *not the helplessness of disease,* but the helplessness of sin. We should picture him to his own conscience, not primarily as infirmity leaning upon infinite strength, but as guilt resting against infinite holiness. We should portray a dependence which can give him no peace so long as he remains impenitent. It should be a dependence which brings together all the elements of God's moral government to intensify the holiness of God on the one hand, and on the other the sinfulness of sin. It should heap the whole burden of sin upon the *sinner's own will.*

Our teaching, then, should be clear and bold in its implications, and if need be in its assertions, of this dependence of guilt, and of guilt only, while impenitence holds out. Our exhortations to an impenitent sinner should imply, and if needful say to him: "You can repent; you can turn to God; you ought to do it; by every principle of equity and of honor, he holds you responsible for doing it; but this is the very head and front of your offending, that you will not do it till his grace constrains you. It depends, therefore, upon his sovereign will whether you shall be saved or lost. The more profound your guilt the more absolute is your dependence; and the more absolute your dependence the more aggravated is your guilt. Each is the gauge of the other. Time consolidates both. Left to yourself, therefore, you must more surely perish, and more hopelessly, than if you could not repent. The climax of your peril is in resistance to the Holy Ghost. Years in ease are years of defiance to infinite holiness. The one sin which shall not be forgiven, neither in this world nor in the world to come, is sin against the Holy Ghost. There is a sin unto death; I do not say that ye should pray for it."

Grace Not Justice

But are not such conceptions of dependence and guilt repellant? Do they not shock hope? Does not such teaching therefore invite despair? Yes, if impenitence be incorrigible. Truth and sin are implacable foes. It is one of the perils of their contact that it may hasten the catastrophe of a soul's ruin. Yet here, again, truth provides its own defences by suggesting all the alleviation of its terrors which can be beneficent to a sinner in his impenitence. Not only are his cavils against the rectitude of God's government silenced, but —

A third result from the principles we have reviewed is, that we are at liberty to proclaim the offer of the Holy Spirit to the sinner as being in unqualified language the gift of God's mercy. We present it not as the gift of justice to necessity; not even as the gift of pity to misfortune; but as the gift of mercy to guilt. Were man's dependence upon God in regeneration a dependence for power to repent, regeneration could be only an act of justice—nothing more. Grace should be no more grace. If we must say to an awakened sinner: "True, you cannot obey God, but the Holy Spirit can enable you to obey; you have no power to repent, but the Holy Spirit can give you repentance; you have no ability to believe, but the Holy Spirit can give you faith;" the reply is inevitable: "Then the gift of the Holy Spirit is my right in equity; I have a claim in eternal justice to regeneration, if commands are laid upon me which I cannot obey without it. Impossible duties are the demand of tyranny." To inquiring minds this reasoning is as resistless as lightning. They are astonished that it does not strike the pulpit dumb.

But we preach the gospel of salvation with no such lurid logic in the background. We are free to proclaim the work of the Holy Ghost as the gift of Mercy to Guilt. Behold what manner of love the Father hath bestowed! While we are yet sinners, grace comes to our deliverance. The sinner in the very act of sin at the very height of rebellion, able to yield, but persistent in treason, with power calling upon guilt and guilt responding to power, is overtaken, enclosed, and subdued by regenerating love. Such is the reach of infinite mercy. Let us be jubilant in proclaiming the gift of the Holy Ghost as a token, superadded to the gift of Christ, of the sincerity of God in his desire to save lost men. Let us exult in the strains of Biblical invitation, promise, expostulation. The gift of the Holy Spirit is proof in act that they mean just what they seem to mean: "Listen, everyone that thirsteth; The Spirit and the Bride say come; Whosoever will, let him come; I have no pleasure in the death of the wicked; Why will ye die?"

Encouragement To Immediate Repentance

But after all, will not such teaching fail through want of individuality in a sinner's faith in it? Will he not say: "True, God is infinitely holy and infinitely merciful; but what is that to me? How do I know that he purposes to regenerate me? Must I not await his time for my salvation? Is not the dependence of guilt just as hopeless as the dependence of necessity? Is not the certainty of sin the certainty of damnation?" Yes; if a sinner will have it so. But truth benignly pursues him even to his selfish isolation in his guilt. For —

A fourth result of the principles we have discussed is, that we are free to assure men that they have every encouragement to immediate repentance which is possible to a state of sin. Holy encouragement is not possible to hope in incorrigible guilt. But a sinner, once convinced of sin, has all the encouragement that he can have to immediate action in the duty of repentance. He has the assurance of the benignity of God's command to repent; of his own ability to obey; of the complacency of God in every desire he cherishes to obey; of the co-working of the Holy Spirit even in every conviction he feels that he ought to obey; of the sincerity of the Spirit in the very pressure of which he is conscious of the motives to obey; and of the possibility that even now the Spirit may overpower his guilt, and make him willing to obey.

Beyond this, holy encouragement cannot extend. No honest soul will ask for more than this. If a sinner accepts other cheer than this, it is because his is not an honest soul. Anything less or more than this simple urgency of immediate duty in reliance upon the Holy Ghost, would only deepen the hopelessness of a sinner in his guilt. No other exhortation comes right home to his emergency as this does: "Work, for God worketh in thee." This is no mockery. It is intensely real, as expressing both God's sincerity and the sinner's duty. The practical force of that much-abused exhortation is simply this: Be in earnest to save yourself, because God is in earnest to save you. Salvation, then, is sure, in the act of instant repentance. This is what the sinner must do to be saved.

But is the inquiry still pressed: Will the Holy Spirit certainly bless my endeavors? We answer: What endeavors? The endeavors of guilt to evade the consciousness of guilt? No. When He the Spirit of truth is come, he will reprove the world of sin. But again, what endeavors? Endeavors to be saved in the indulgence of sin? No: the fruit of the Spirit is in all goodness and righteousness and truth. But again, what endeavors?

Endeavors to fasten the responsibility of sin and its fruits upon the sovereignty of God's decrees? No, but who are you, O man, that replies against God? Yet again, what endeavors? The endeavors of an earnest spirit to believe and love and obey? Thus saith the high and lofty One who inhabits eternity, whose name is Holy "I dwell with him that is of a contrite and humble spirit."

But does a sinner say: "Mine is not a contrite spirit; can I then be assured that God will give me repentance? Is that irreversible decree, formed before the world was, anywhere revealed to me that, taking me just as I am, God will change my heart?" We answer, No. God gives no such assurance. He reveals no such decrees. He has no answer to give to such inquiry. We listen, as that cry goes up to the throne of mercy, and there is silence in heaven. We hear no responses in the air; we see no handwriting in the clouds. He hath mercy on whom he will have mercy:

"Not Gabriel asks the reason why,
    Nor God the reason gives."

This is the point precisely to which the whole bearing of our instructions should conduct men in their search for peace to their souls — that they stand face to face with God, dependent for eternal life upon his good pleasure, with every possible encouragement, even to the assurance of salvation, in instant obedience to his commands, and with nothing but despair in disobedience or in delay. What God purposes to do respecting the regeneration of any soul he has not revealed to any mortal ear. He does not ask our attention nor invite our inquiries to that secret of his own will. He urges upon our thoughts our own doing; what we have done, what we must do. There is no secret about that; it is open and clear as the morning.

The Ruin of a Soul its Own Work

But what if such proclamation of the gospel fails? What if its only fruit is to awaken the lamentation: "To whom is the arm of the Lord revealed?" Even then, truth is its own vindication, and the ways of God are equal. For —

The final consequence from the principles we have contemplated is, that we should represent a sinner's destruction to be always his own doing. We may be called to portray the history of the Holy Spirit's work on many souls in the words once dropped in tears over Jerusalem: "How often would I . . . but ye would not." Our teaching should be, that it does not extenuate a lost sinner's guilt that God never decreed to regenerate him. Where is the sinner's claim to that decree? Not in defect of responsibility; that has been without fracture from the first to the last. Not in default of knowledge; his knowledge and his duty have but measured each other. Not in bondage of probation; his probation never rose above the level of his freedom. Not in severity of temptation; temptation at its floodtide was but opportunity for more blessed achievement. His liberty to obey God's commands was infinitely more sacred in God's sight than in his own. Never was its awful sanctity suspended or overborne for one moment. God has guarded it as the apple of his eye. To no being in the universe, then, is the perdition of a sinner to be primarily ascribed but to himself.

But this is not all. We must proclaim the history of a lost soul in words of more intense significance. That is not a history of negative probation. God has never thrust a sinner upon trial in the sheer strength of his freedom, and let him alone. God has been more than just to him. By the very conditions of his being, the sinner has been the object of all the amiable affections of the Divine nature. He has been placed upon an infinitely beneficent system of trial. He has been instructed in all that God has held him accountable for; his own intuitions have taught him; the works of God have enlightened him; his own conscience has been the foreshadow of the judgment to him; there has never been an hour of his moral being when he did not know enough for his salvation. Everything that he has known of God has assumed also the benign form of a dissuasive from sin; his experience has generated countless motives to obedience; his steps have been thronged by them as by pleading spirits; but for his guilt, his conscience alone would have been an ever present song of God's love to him; if he has had Christian training, the disclosures of redemption have opened upon him the most intense system of allurements to holiness known to the universe; the teachings of wise men, the prayers of good men, the visions of inspired men, and the ministrations of angels, have stretched a cordon of holy sympathies around him; the cross of Christ has blocked his way to destruction more impassably than by a flaming sword; intercession in heaven has been made for him with hands uplifted in which were the prints of the nails;

the Holy Spirit has striven with him to turn him back, by all the devices which infinite ingenuity could frame at the bidding of infinite compassion; his history has been one long struggle against obstacles to the suicide of his soul; silently, darkly, often with conscious and wilful repugnance to holy restraints, yet as often with that adroit suspense of conscience with which a sinner may serenely, even joyously, fraternize with sin, he has sought out, and discovered, and selected, and seized upon, and made sure of, his own way over and around and through those obstacles, to the world of despair. He has done it — he, and not another. Such is every lost life. Is it any marvel that a lost soul is speechless?

Chapter 5

The Indwelling of the Holy Spirit

It is one of the perils of probation that the most stupendous truths may become the least impressive. In religious thought such are the truths with which we become most familiar; and through our familiarity with them, our intellects may grow drowsy over them and through the dulness of our conceptions our hearts may become torpid in response to them. By a subtle law of language the words which express such truths may become tame. Intense words, once the utterance of an intense experience, may lose their heat; figurative words, originated to express vivid ideas which could not otherwise be pressed into language, may die out in literal commonplace. We may read and speak and pray, therefore, as we may think, of some of the grandest ideas of our faith, without emotion, because without a lifelike sense of their reality. They may become that which we so significantly describe as "a dead letter." An apostolic earnestness, admonishing us of such a truth, may startle, us into a momentary vision of it, by addressing us as if we had lost our faith in it; as if we had sunk into ignorance of its existence. "Know ye not?" may be the query which hints at the deadness of our sensibility.

Let us seek to quicken our thoughts of one of these well-known elements of Christian truth, by observing some of the lessons suggested by the Indwelling of the Holy Spirit in regenerate souls. "Know ye not that ye are the Temple of God, and that the Spirit of God dwelleth in you?"

I. THE SACREDNESS OF A CHRISTIAN'S BEING

The work of the Holy Ghost in regeneration suggests with singular impressiveness, the sacredness of a Christian's being. A renewed mind is a consecrated thing. It is sacred as the abode of God. In all history, a temple has been an object of reverence as the dwelling-place of Deity. Men close its doors against profane intrusion. They put off their shoes and approach it with prostrations. The ground on which it has stood has been deemed holy. The very soil within its courts has been carried over seas as a memorial of divine virtues. By human law, crime has been sometimes so gauged as to reach its climax in an act of sacrilege. The avenger of blood, in hot pursuit of the murderer, has stopped short on the threshold of a sanctuary, lest by entering with vengeful purpose he should commit a worse crime than that which he sought to punish.

Such a Temple of God is a regenerate soul. The thoughts of such a soul may be the radiation of the thoughts of God. Its emotions may be tremulous with the sensibility of God. Its purposes may be decrees of the Will of God. Its entire character may be a similitude of the holiness of God. Its life, therefore, may be the life of God, and its joy the peace of God. A man may have reason to stand in awe of himself. He may be an object of reverence to an observant universe, as a being who is filled with the fulness of God. This is Christian privilege. Realized in experience or not, the Christian prerogative towers to this height.

So inspired men measured a regenerate life by the very name by which they distinguished one who had experienced the new birth. Why should our modern speech have dropped the title of "saint," in designating a converted man? Why should it sound eccentric to our ears that a quaint Christian like George Müller should speak of ministering to the "saints of Bristol?" That conception of a holy thing, of a sacred being, of a soul set apart by a Godlike initiation to Godlike uses, is the scriptural idea of the humblest friend of Christ.

No fear of an affected sanctimony should repel us from this ideal of a soul's hallowed affinity with God. No deference to an earthly dialect should forbid us to honor this ideal as a reality in our speech. The dignity of a soul culminates in this conception. The diction of the Scriptures is full of it. We are kings; we are priests; we are the elect of God; we are saints of the Most High; we are judges of angels; we are joint-heirs with Christ. These homelike verities of our Christian vows are not a farce; because we are the Temple of God. In his view of us, the light of his own mind irradiates, and the benignity of his own heart enkindles our being. Therefore it is that the meanest of us all are precious to him. Whoso touches us touches the apple of his eye. He that offends one of us, it were better for him that a millstone were hanged about his neck, and he were cast into the sea.

The Indwelling of the Spirit Not an Incarnation

We do not hold a mystical interpretation of God's indwelling. That is not necessary; nor indeed does it help us to reduce to an experience our conception of the enshrinement of God in a human soul. We must not part with nor confound the sense of our own individuality. We need not struggle to assimilate our union with God to that of the union of Deity with the man Jesus. The residence of God in a contrite heart is not an incarnation of Divinity. We need not strain the figurative speech of inspiration, so as to derive from it the notion of some sort of essential union of which we can form no definite idea. We neither dignify nor intensify our thought of the abiding of God with us by any such struggle. We materialize it rather, and so degrade it.

The expression of God by the act of personal Deity is all that we can know of his presence anywhere. What more than this can we know of his omnipresence in the material creation? Wherever a Divine thought is, there is the mind of God. Wherever an outgoing of Divine love occurs, there is the heart of God. Wherever a Divine energy works, there is the will of God. We know nothing of effluences of the Divine Essence. Be it in a star or in a soul, God is wherever there is an expression of his perfections. Differing in glory, indeed, as one star from another, and as a spirit in God's image transcends both, yet the Divine emanations are from one Being, whose expression of himself in any form, and in minutest degree, is sufficient to hallow a locality or to consecrate a soul.

The sacredness of an expression of God exists, also, only to the mind which thinks it. The Shekinah was no hallowed thing to the bullock which stood up for sacrifice; but a ladder in a man's dream could transform a field of almond-trees into a Bethel, and a pillow of stones into an altar, at which the dreamer should say, trembling: "How dreadful is this place! The Lord is here and I knew it not!" So, one flower in the desert of Sahara, blooming forth its expression of the benevolence of Him who from eternity had purposed that it should there and then be a memorial of that benevolence to Mungo Park, could render that spot like the gate of heaven.

In like manner, then, a regenerate soul, as the habitation of a sanctifying influence, becomes a temple of the Holy Ghost no less really than if the very essence of the Deity were incarnate in the body which encloses that soul. We speak the wisdom of God in a mystery. Such a soul is sacred to holy uses. It may be contracted in its range of intellect; but to the eye of God it is a chosen shrine. It may be low in the scale of human birth; yet it is more than the kindred of angels. A slave it may be by human law, and yet a son of the King of kings. That scarred body in which it dwells is a consecrated thing; the death of it is precious in the Lord's sight. Whoso defiles that temple of God, him will God destroy.

II. THE RESTORATION OF LOST SELF-RESPECT

The residence of the Holy Spirit in a renewed heart discloses, furthermore, the only method by which a sinner may honestly recover a sense of personal dignity.

The Tyranny of Remorse

It is one of the evil incidents of guilt that a man loses himself by it. Confidence in his own integrity, complacency in his own history, esteem for his own worth, trust in his own honor, assurance of his own dignity, joy in his own conscience,—all the chivalrous emotions by which a pure being is permitted to exult in the very consciousness of existence,—are swept away by the first breath of sin felt to be sin. An unholy man, as such, can no more honor himself than Satan can. Guilt must be painted before it can look its own image in the eye. It must be dressed gaudily with disguises before it can hold up its head and walk loftily. A guilty man must cheat himself before he can respect himself. This he cannot do under the espionage of a remorseful conscience. Remorse is hawk-eyed and savagely honest. It searches everywhere, sees everything, keeps nothing back. It is more pitiless than death. A sinner enthralled by it can neither bear it nor brave it. He must be crushed by the consciousness of degradation. He must live in self-abhorrence.

If this were not so, extreme guilt might be saved from the extreme of punishment. A man, however depraved, might bear the brunt of a world's loathing, if he could be raised above self-loathing. Is it not conceivable that Judas Iscariot might be calm under the execrations of the universe, if he could stupefy the consciousness of deserving them? We cannot be assured that Omnipotence can crush incorrigible guilt otherwise than by forms of retribution which shall compel it to know itself.

From this "lower deep" underneath the "lowest," in which a sinner feels, as Milton's Satan did, "Myself am hell," a sinner needs deliverance.

We all need it. If we have never felt by anticipation this tyranny of Remorse, so surely as we are sinners unforgiven, it is lurking for us in the future, like an assassin in the dark, and we need a rescue. How shall we obtain it? How shall we get back a consciousness of something in us which we shall dare to honor? Without such a consciousness, immortality, which we crave so thirstily, must become an intolerable burden, and nowhere of more leaden weight than in heaven. How shall we recover a self-knowledge which can endure eternity?

Can pride restore it? The pride of Satan does not hope for so much as that. The first honest hour we have when we are brought face to face with God, will disclose to us that pride is one of the meanest of the mental vices; the most contracted, the most selfish, and the most false-hearted; and therefore the first to betray a man to despair, and the most eager and relentless in heaping upon him shame and everlasting contempt. The facts of life discover a subtle affinity between pride and suicide.

The Discoveries of a Pure Conscience

But what is the working of the soul in its introspection, when once opened to the ingress of the Holy Spirit?

Is there no re-awakening of self-respect, when the evidence of that Divine presence first becomes clear to consciousness? The cleansing blood of Christ, once made a reality to faith by the illumining grace of God, — can one get no buoyancy of heart from that? The dropping off of the soul's corruptions, the fading away of its "guilty stains," under the discipline of the Sanctifier, —cannot one derive from that process, however gradual, some new sense of dignity? The blotting out of the past from the record of conscience; the opening of a fresh, clean page for the future reckoning; the first throbbing life, however infantile, of that which the Scriptures call a *"pure* conscience,"—can one find in these no ground of hope that one may yet become an object of one's own esteem?

In that awful and yet precious alliance with Godhead, we are raised to think the thoughts of God. We are invited to share in the benign sympathies of God. We are welcome to execute in our own intensified individuality, and yet in dear subjection to his bidding, the purposes of God. We are assured that He does not deem himself degraded by his union with us. From eternity he has chosen us to this. Before the geologic cycles began, he had us in his thoughts for this. With clear foresight of our disgusting guilt, he did not waver in the choice. When he repented that he had made man upon the earth, our names were engravers upon the palm of his hand. Through all the ages that have come and gone, he has held us faithfully in mind. His experience of our waywardness has never turned his loving eye from us. His royal decree towards us has run in this one groove, without variableness or shadow of turning. And now, in the fulness of time, when that decree approaches its consummation, he condescends to think it honorable to that glory which the heaven of heavens cannot contain, to abide with us, even with us, with the meanest and most guilty of us, to dwell within us, to work in us his own good pleasure, to the intent that even by us should be made known his wisdom unto principalities and powers. In all this, is not some foundation laid for the rebuilding of that consciousness of worth which we have lost? Shall we not dare at length to respect that which God has thus ennobled? Who shall lay anything to the charge of God's elect?

True, it requires great faith to appropriate this dignity to ourselves. Self-abasement may often struggle with the assurance of this Divine indwelling. Said a dying Christian to a friend, "I sent for you to tell you how happy I am. I did not think it possible for a man to enjoy so much of God on earth. I never asked for joy; I always thought myself unworthy of it; but he has given me more than I asked. It seems as if it cannot be for me; as if it must be for somebody else; I do not deserve it. I am filled with God. I know that he is in me, and I in him. I shall see him as he is. I delight in knowing that." Thus, even in a saint whose vision is a foresight of heaven, faith may have to struggle into consciousness of his own grandeur; but the grandeur is none the less real for that.

What shall we then say to these things? If God be for us, who can be against us? We are more than conquerors through him that loved us. Here is ground for self-esteem which has no root of arrogance. We only honor that which God has honored. Self-abasement and self-complacency here go hand in hand. "Not unto us, not unto us?" we say, yet in the same breath we add: "Now are we the sons of God, and what we shall be doth not yet appear."

Courage in the Day of Judgment

Have we not often imagined that redeemed souls must have a strange meeting at the judgment, when the secrets of hearts shall be revealed? Is the prospect of it altogether welcome to us? It has been said that, if in this world every man's heart could be open to the gaze of every other man, no two could ever again be friends, for no two could look each other in the eye. How, then, will our self-respect bear the last ordeal? The beloved apostle gives us the answer. "God dwelleth in us. Hereby know we that we dwell in him, and he in us, because he hath given us of his Spirit. We know that when he shall appear, we shall be like him. Herein is our love made perfect, that we may have boldness in the day of judgment, because as he is so are we." If we indeed know this, why should we not be bold?

In that day, we shall revere in others the clear image of God, wrought by God's own hand. They will revere the same in us. We shall meet each other without a blush. Some of our departed kindred have been glorified so long before us, that we are apt to think of them as vastly our superiors. Their distance from us, which years are lengthening, disheartens us. But we shall overtake them, and that will be no crestfallen meeting. We shall receive their welcome without confusion. We shall not fear their secret contempt when they take us by the hand. Their greetings will have no hollow sound. The salutations of angels will not abash us. The morning stars, which exult in a sinless history of thousands of years, will not look chillingly upon us. Gabriel, Michael, the seven spirits before the throne, will not recognize us haughtily. Even the eye of the Infinite One will not close itself in disgust at our appearing. It shall search us, — He that formed the eye, shall not he see? — it shall search us indeed, but as light searches a prism. It shall find only itself reflected at every angle, and in a radiance of beauty which nothing but itself could evoke.

III. Intensity Of Regenerate Life

If such be the dignity to which a regenerate soul attains through the presence and working of God within it, it is further obvious that the tendency of renewed character must be to manifest itself in intense forms of experience.

It is a law of all nature, that vigorous forces shall act themselves out. We look for results proportioned to the power which produces them. Do we not expect that fire will burn, that light will be visible, that thunder will be audible, and that lightning will leave a mark where it strikes? The most latent elements lead to a disclosure of themselves. Any great energy in nature, however breathless in its operation, must sooner or later be discovered. Electricity could not forever hide itself from detection by some one of the human senses. Even while undetected in itself, the electric force must work, and its working be visible in results. So much power, — so much product, is the law.

Why should not the same law hold good in the spiritual world? Shall infinite perfection express itself, and seem to find the blessedness of its being in self-expression, in all things elsewhere, and yet find no egress through the human spirit which is so like it? It surely must be the law of God's working in a soul, to become manifest to observers. Such a power must act itself out in unequivocal effects.

Latent Piety Unnatural
The tendencies of regenerate beings, then, must be averse to concealment. Christian character absolutely latent in a soul would be an anomaly among the works of God. It must tend to, not only self-expression, but to great positiveness of evidence. The law of its being is to be self-evident. A renewed mind is naturally a transparent being through whom the holiness of God reflects itself in human graces. If such positive evidence of piety do not appear, a presumption is established that the piety itself does not exist. True, God will not quench the smoking flax, but he will enkindle it. It is not the nature of anything that is on fire to smoulder forever; if it is a living fire, it will burn into a flame. So the life of God in the soul must tend to intensity of development.

The most intense life ever lived on this earth should naturally be a life energized by the Holy Ghost. In such a life the intellect may experience a marvellous awakening. The tendency of its working is to the positiveness of knowledge. Probabilities grow to certainties in the convictions of such a mind. Belief becomes assurance. The range of intellectual vision expands as the soul ascends the mount of its transfiguration. Dr. Chalmers was an accomplished astronomer when he was the unconverted pastor of Kilmany; but the world did not know it. Why? Because the power of the "Astronomical Discourses" was not in him then.

Even an inferior intellect becomes, through the quickening of profound sensibilities by the indwelling of God, susceptible of exertions which make men honorable among men. There is a wonderful educating force in the working of grace upon the most unpromising natures. John Howard was not constitutionally a man of commanding intellect. The

universities of England despised him, for he was not of them. It was his
life-long affliction that he could not write a letter of considerable length
with an assurance of its grammatical accuracy. But when the indwelling
of God had wrought in him, the world found him out and now is proud
of him.

Is Regenerate Experience Fanatical?

In this view, there is nothing singular in the charge of fanaticism upon
a regenerated man. Such a man, acting out obediently the power which
is within him, will never escape that charge, in one form or another, till
the world is filled with such fanatics. It was not much learning, it was
much grace, that made Paul seem a madman to Festus. "As for Chalmers,
he is mad" — so said the noble ones of Scotland when that voice, as of
one crying in the wilderness, began to be beard from the solitude of Kilmany. It has been said "of all great workers and thinkers of the world,"
that their power is a "force as of madness, in the hands of reason." Vastly
more significant is this of the "power of an endless life," awakened and
girded through the union of a soul with the Infinite Mind.

We may test, therefore, by this criterion, diverse types of professedly
Christian experience. Many such offer themselves to our observation in
real life; which of them exhibits, by its intensity, the keenest sympathy
with the working of an infinite power in the soul? One ideal of Christian
character invites to a life of self-indulgence. Surely, the indwelling of God
never originated that. Another conception of the Christian faith degrades
it to a gauge of respectability in society, or of refinement in culture. Is
it possible that the witness of the Holy Ghost has ever testified to that?

A certain model of Christian profession is remarkable for its effemi-
nacy. It represents one who is ashamed to speak, and who cannot labor
and dare not suffer, for Christ. He assumes the reality of a latent godliness. His reticent speech proclaims only the secrecy of religion as an
affair between the soul and God. His theory of life, his social habits, the
companionship he seeks, the amusements he approves, his uses of prop-
erty, of time, of culture, and of mental gifts, all tend to obliterate the
distinction between the church and the world, between "saint" and "sinner." In all those things which would make godliness visible to observers,
he approaches as near to a "world lying in wickedness" as he can approach without arousing that world's contempt for him as a hypocrite.
Is it conceivable that such a model of a Christ-like life was ever wrought

by the "exceeding greatness of God's power"? Did the Spirit ever help our infirmities with groanings which cannot be uttered, to evoke such an ideal from the depths of our souls? Has it ever cost a man strong crying and tears to execute it?

From such a type of Christianity it is but a step to that represented by one who can ridicule Christian missions in their inception, admire the romance of them in their progress, and pour unctuous adulations upon their success; who is always in sympathy with the world in its caricatures of Christian doctrine; who can amuse himself alike with nicknames of Christian revivals, with jeers at Christian reforms, and with burlesques of Christian men. Can it be that an Infinite Mind is dwelling, thinking, feeling, working in that little soul? We can, discern the handiwork of God in the brain of a butterfly; his work there, is apposite to the thing he works upon. But who can discover any traces of God, in such a model of Christian character?

When God works in a human spirit he works as he did when he created that spirit. He produces something which is like himself. He quickens into being a thing which expresses itself in a Godlike way. He inspires a character which is built on intense convictions, which take possession of a man, and which claim and use the whole of him. Such convictions, wielded by such a Power, make life earnest, because they make Eternity real and God absolute. Nothing else grates so harshly against the grain of a regenerate nature as to be either a hypocrite or but half a man in religious life. The germ of a martyr is in every soul which God has chosen as his abode. Humble and contrite, indeed, is the spirit with which he dwells, but under his reviving lofty and jubilant as the morning; Weak, faint, cast down, ready to perish, it may be; but in his strength a conqueror. Sensitive to suffering, timid in peril, a woman in delicacy of nerve, a child in resolution, it has often been; but through communion with an infinite Friend, it has become so possessed with the consciousness of spiritual life and the assurance of a blessed immortality, that it has seen no terrors in death, none in torture. Such souls have reserved their fears for something more appalling than these. This intensity of regenerate life has made martyrs of Christian children.

IV. WORKING OF THE SPIRIT BY DISCOVERABLE LAWS

Such paradoxes of holy experience as we have just observed are not contradictions. They are not even anomalies. Marvellous as they seem to observers, inexplicable as they appeal to minds which are oblivious of the Divine energy in them, they are but the normal results of the dwelling of God in tried souls. We should therefore observe further, *the dependence of the growth of regenerate character upon conformity to the laws of the Holy Spirit's working.*

In ascribing laws to the process by which a soul is sanctified, we only affirm the oneness of God. We only assume that in spiritual operations he works, in this respect, as he does in nature. In the one as in the other, Law is the expression of the very mind of God. Caprice can find no lodgment in an infinite Will. An arbitrary act can surely find no more place in the redemption of a soul than in the creation of light.

But are the laws of spiritual agency in a regenerate mind discoverable? Certainly, so far as their discovery can be serviceable to their success. True, Divine energy in the new birth is likened to the wind; but even the wind, in the very phenomenon of its blowing where it listeth and hiding the whence and the whither, yields up to wise observation some of the laws which govern its apparent vagaries. So is everyone that is born of the Spirit. Some of the laws of the Holy Ghost reveal themselves among the first lessons of a regenerate life. They lie open for inspection, also, in certain injunctions of the Scriptures.

The Law Of Harmony With Other Revelations Of God
It surely may be accepted as a law of the working of the Spirit in the soul, that its teachings will harmonize with other revelations of God. God cannot contradict God. God in Creation, God in Providence, God in His revealed Word, will confirm the witness of the Spirit in the heart which he has hallowed as his Temple. To a docile mind which is watching for a disclosure of the Divine Will, there is often an overpowering reciprocity of evidence which leaves no room for a doubt. One stands as in the focus of an amphitheatre of mountains, in which one hears from all sides the reverberations of a single voice. It is as if, by some mysterious law of infinite being, the Divine mind held communion with itself through the medium of the faculties of a man. That voice seems to be his own — it is his own, and yet another's.

Hence it is that those Christians who give evidence of being most profoundly moved by the Spirit of God, are those who most reverently study the word and the providences of God. They expect one revelation of the Infinite Mind to give answer to another. They interpret the one by the response of the other. They tread softly, listening for the echo from without to the intimation within. Such Christians do not become wrongheaded nor drivelling believers. They are not suffered often to mistake a wayward fancy or a whiff of self-conceit for a divine impulse in their souls. They do not see visions nor dream dreams. Their faith and their good sense grow abreast with each other.

The Law Of Harmony With The Nature Of Mind

Is it not an equally positive law of the Holy Spirit's working, that it moves in and through the natural laws of the soul itself? It creates no new elements of mind. It introduces no new principles of mental action. It is simply one work of God within another. It is a Spirit energizing a spirit. Divine influence transfuses itself through the natural operations of human intellect, of human sensibilities, and of human will, so delicately in the process, and so evenly in the result, that the mind is unconscious of any other efficiency than its own. Divine indwelling does not disclose itself as such to the consciousness of the believer, as electricity does not display its presence as such in the sensations of the healthy body which it pervades. The kingdom of God in the soul cometh not with observation.

Sanctification is not to be looked for, therefore, in shocks of spasmodic piety. It is not to be discovered by dissecting one's own being in search of Him who is past finding out. It is not to be augmented by stimulating devotional fervor into turbulence. From passionate prayer the soul, by a necessity of its nature, must sink back into apathy.

Such vibration between extremes is a very different phenomenon from that which is so generally witnessed in profound Christian experience, and which expresses itself in the sense of *conflict*. Probationary discipline necessarily involves struggle. Besides conflicts with sin, known and felt to be sin, a renewed soul may have struggles with infirmity, through which a holy life may sometimes become a life of strong crying and tears. Then it is, especially, that the Spirit helps us. Yet even this, if it becomes habitual, evinces disproportion in the growth of regenerate experience. Two very similar distortions may induce it. One is a disproportion of

intellect; the other a disproportion of sensibility. Let intellectual conceptions of God gain a large overgrowth upon the outgoings of the heart to
him in love; or let sensibility to the Divine presence outgrow intelligence
of the Divine character; in either case, the being of the man becomes
disjointed. It works unequally and inconstantly. His progress is full of
breaks and delays in which his struggle is not with sin consciously in-
dulged, but simply with the obliquity of his mental habits. His soul
yearns to recover its lost equipoise. An old legend reads that a saint once
longed and fasted and prayed for a vision of God which should equal his
seraphic ardor. But when the archangel took him and carried him swiftly
up through the immensity of space, he began to tremble, and cried out
for relief from the intolerable sense of God's infinity.

The Holy Spirit is more kindly considerate of our infirmities than we
ourselves sometimes are. He does not call them sins. And yet the most
finished experience of the Divine indwelling balances, and at length
rectifies them. It quiets painful vibrations. It acts as a sedative to spasms
of godliness. It is emphatically the very life of God in the soul. It tends
to make a man like God; and His being is not made up of alternations
between ecstasy and despair. Such an equable force of vitality will evince
itself in an experience which resembles the throb of a calm, strong,
healthy heart. The Scriptures symbolize it by a well of water—the most
refreshing thing in Nature; a perennial thing; not stagnant yet not boisterous; transparent and spontaneous; springing up in the morning and
at noon and at eventide and in the night watches.

It should be remembered, therefore, that in religious life, as in other
developments of character, the most intense minds are not the most
turbulent. God's presence is their natural atmosphere, in which they live
and move and have their being tranquilly, because with an intensity
which acts through the natural forces of character, and pervades them
all alike. Hence it is that the noblest of renewed men have been men of
the most generous range of graces. The manly and the feminine virtues,
the contemplative and the active, the massive and the minute, the impul-
sive and the circumspect, have been intertwined in symmetry. The beauty
of the Lord our God has been upon them. Christ had no eccentricities.
He had not even those of genius, of which the world is so tolerant. Yet
what other life has been so intense as his?

The Law of Co-operation

We cannot mistake in recognizing as in the law of the Holy Spirit, that his work shall be concurrent with the will of the regenerate soul itself. Sanctification is a co-operative process. It may be suspended by resistance, and accelerated by obedience to the Divine impulses. The Spirit may be "grieved" by the desecration of the temple he has chosen. There is a reason in the nature of his work for that fearful admonition: "Quench not the Spirit." What more affecting exhibition is conceivable of the condescension of God, than this mystery of forbearance, in which the Holy Ghost stands as if in waiting upon the choices of the poor, guilty sufferer whom he yearns to save? What a glimpse, too, of the reach of the responsibility of a regenerate soul, of its dignities and, its perils, is here!

Not by the breadth of a hair will the sovereignty of God invade the enclosure of that soul's freedom. The soul itself, in its own individuality, is the thing he would save. Its own love is the thing he craves. Its own submission is the right he claims. Its own chosen obedience is the service he requires. Its own heart is the gift he stoops to ask for.

For aught that we know, God could translate that lost soul up to the group of the presence-angels and make a Gabriel of it. But this would not be, in the Divine estimate of things, so noble an achievement of Power, as to win that soul just as it is, in its feebleness, in its diminutive, human, fallen being, — to allure it by the infinite ingenuity of love to give itself away to him willingly. Nothing less than this will satisfy the generosity of Christ. This, therefore, is adopted as a principle governing the operations of the Spirit — that holiness shall be a man's own choice. He shall have all that he wills to have. Blessed is he if he hungers and thirsts for it, for he shall be filled.

Hence the Scriptures teach just what Christian experience proves — that Christian development advances in the line of Christian duties. He shall have it in most affluent increase who uses most diligently what he has. To him that hath shall be given. The power of a life hid with Christ is not to be hoped for in either an indolent or a despondent waiting for a Divine afflatus. Supernatural influence coming to a man in such conditions of soul is more likely to be from below than from above. Graces come in groups to the soul that is open and receptive of Divine suggestions. They throng around him who is watching for them in the way of duty. A wise man's eagerness to be like God will expend itself in doing for God. So much obedience — so much growth; this is the law. God worketh in you—therefore work ye; this is the charge.

The Law of Sanctification by Prayer

In the same line of thought, is it not equally certain that a law of gracious energy in the soul makes its growth dependent on the expression of its desires in trustful prayer? True, the desire itself must be inspired by the very Being who is its object; yet this is the method of an unsearchable wisdom. The interchanges of fellowship between a renewed mind and its Divine Guest are very wonderful. Herein is the mystery of communion with God. We talk of it glibly, but how little do we know of it! He quickens desire in his regenerate friend, that he may gratify it; and he gratifies the desire that he may augment it by indulgence; so that it may express itself again, to be gratified anew. Prayer, and response prompting again to prayer, to be again responded to—thus the life that is hid with Christ in God unfolds itself in the consciousness of the believer. It is a sublime antiphony between heaven and earth, to which he is the only listener. The Scriptures speak in terms of awful familiarity of the inter-communion of God and godly men. Enoch walked with God, and was not, for God took him. Abraham was the friend of God. What is the meaning of that soliloquy over the plains of Sodom? "Shall I aide from Abraham that thing which I do?" It is as if Jehovah condescends to say: "Abraham is my friend; he has given me his confidence; I have admitted him into affectionate fellowship; and now, is it honorable to conceal from him my purpose towards his kindred?" Who, again, was the nameless friend of Jacob? We are told that "there wrestled a man with him till the breaking of the day." Could any symbol express the intimacy of equals more forcibly than that old story of the Athletes in the field of Peniel? Yet, when the sun rose, Jacob said: "I have seen God, face to face." Go up with Moses into the thick darkness where God dwells, and hear God speaking to him as a man speaks to his friend. Who is He that says of David, as one of us would speak of the friend dearest to us: "He is a man after my own heart"? What indeed is the significance of the Incarnation, in this respect, but that of an expression of God's desire to come down into the homes and hearts of men, to restore to them the holy freedom of Eden in which his voice was heard in the cool of the day? Listen to the benediction which is wafted over the whole world of believers: "I call you not servants, but friends; I have chosen you; I will send the Comforter unto you; He shall abide with you; Ask and you shall receive, that your joy may be full."

Here then we reach the culmination of the history of man's communion with the Godhead. It is in this gift of the Holy Spirit, who descends to dwell with men on terms of holy and yet familiar friendship. No law of Christian growth, therefore, is more pertinent than that of its dependence on the expression of Christian desire in trustful prayer. As prayer is, so is the condition of the soul's union with God. A growing piety will be sensible of this instinctively. A regenerate soul in which the work of grace is not suspended will pray, simply because it may pray. Prayer will be to such a one a homelike, childlike intercourse of friend with friend. The indwelling of God invites to this kind of prayer, and renders all ideas of prayer which are incongruous with this absurd.

Regenerate experience exhibits in this respect an impressive divergence from that of impenitence. Nothing else discloses as prayer does that extreme guilt and eminent godliness are at opposite poles of spiritual life. There is a degree of guilt in which a man can conceive of nothing else so appalling to him as the thought of asking a blessing from God. That thought brings God too near.

Men in despair, on death-beds, have writhed with redoubled anguish when urged to beg for Divine mercy. "Do not name prayer to me," said Thomas Paine, in his last hours. By a terrible law of retribution, a soul abandoned by the Holy Spirit starts back, shuddering, from the idea of the lost possibility of his friendship. It is like one in a frightful dream, who cannot shout for help, and who is in the more frantic agony because he cannot.

But to one in whom the indwelling of God is deepening and expanding, so that be at length becomes, like Stephen, full of the Holy Ghost, prayer becomes an habitual joy, like any other habit of sacred friendship. Only to such a man is the poetic ideal of prayer lifelike — that it is a "Christian's vital breath," his "native air." John Foster, on his death-bed, observing that his strength was fast leaving him, said: "But I can pray, and that is a glorious thing." The glory of the thing is very apt to loom up in the soul's vision as it approaches heaven.

The Law of Trust in a Divine Plan

Once more, is it not also a law of the Holy Spirit which is vital to Christian growth, that his work in the renewed soul is carried on by a plan which will be consummated? It has no contingencies unknown to God or not provided for in his purposes. The entire process is part of a system of decrees. It is enclosed and embedded in a plan of which no eye has ever seen the beginning, and none will ever see the end.

For the most symmetrical Christian growth, therefore, our hopes and methods of Christian culture need to be constructed upon faith in sanctification as being, not only a practicable achievement, but a result which is fixed by everlasting purposes. It should be a reality to us that we have been, and are, and shall be in the thoughts and in the heart of God forever and forever. We may conceive of this as "election," "decree," "eternal purpose;" whatever we name it in our theology, it is simply the execution of a plan which was never a novelty and will never be obsolete in the Divine Mind. God has no caprices about it, and no after-thoughts.

We need to *individualize* his faith by appropriating the object of it, each soul to itself. We need this for the comfort of it. We need it more for the courage it gives, and the equanimity of effort which it inspires. Doubt weakens, fear disarms, in a spiritual conflict, as in any other. Why should it not be so? But an experience which is built upon faith in the eternal fidelity of God's friendship promotes a buoyant piety. It stimulates Christian character to a rapid and even expansion. It awakens exultation in the individuality of the soul's union with God. A living psalmist has feelingly expressed this phase of Christian life in song:

Yes, for me, for me He careth
  With a brother's tender care;
Yes, with me, with me He shareth
  Every burden, every fear.

Yes, o'er me, o'er me He watcheth,
  Ceaseless watcheth, night and day;
Yes, even me, even me He snatcheth
  From the perils of the way.

Yes, in me, in me He dwelleth;
  I in him and He in me
And my empty soul He filleth,
  Here and through eternity.

Thus I wait for his returning,
   Singing all the way to Heaven
Such the joyful song of morning,
   Such the tranquil song of even.

It requires great faith, indeed, to appropriate thus to ourselves the liberty of Christian joy. But surely that is not a Christlike humility which esteems piety in proportion to the distrust it cherishes of one's own salvation. One who can say honestly with the apostle: "I know that He is able to keep that which I have committed unto him," will have much of the Pauline vigor of character in other respects. The mind of such a man will have strong affinities with Light. Joy will be his native element. Genial and cheering views of truth will be the spontaneous expression of his strength. He can hold such views close to his own conscience, a sinner though he be, because he has a history of reverent familiarity with God, in which his soul has learned the secret of sympathy with the blessedness of God.

Index

CPSIA information can be obtained at www.ICGtesting.com
Printed in the USA
BVOW071936071211

277837BV00002B/89/P